Ancient Stones
Timeless
Encouragement

The Encouragers Christian Writers Group

Compiled and edited by Cathy Biggerstaff

Published by EA Books Publishing a division of
Living Parables of Central Florida, Inc. a 501c3
EABooksPublishing.com

A STONE OF WITNESS

We lovingly dedicate this book to:

God, in thanks for the talent, life experiences, and wisdom He brought to each of us. Without Him none of this dream would have been possible. May our Savior receive all the glory for what is accomplished through the words He's given us.

Linda Tomblin, author, teacher, mentor, and friend for starting this writing group on June 28, 2010, and for the critiques and guidance that made us better writers than we thought we could ever be. Thank you, Linda!

All the encouragers, family, friends and fellow writers, who have helped us pen what God put on our hearts. Without your patience and presence in our lives, this book would have remained merely a dream.

Welcome, Dear Readers-

Ancient stones dot the landscape in Israel. Who placed them there and why?

During Old Testament times it was the practice of the people to stand a stone on its edge or pile up many stones as a place to worship God. As the people traveled and life happened, just as it does today, they would encounter times when they didn't feel close to God.

As a remedy, they would return to the last stone they erected. They knew that God had been real to them in that place. It was like a charging station where they could reconnect with God. They reasoned: if God was real here, and they knew he had been; and if He is the same yesterday, today and tomorrow; then He is real where I live now.

Some folks feel like the words of the Old Testament are outdated and not relevant to life today. Did God waste His breath breathing those words into the scribe's soul so they could be recorded? We believe those ancient words are alive and hold meaning for us today.

Come along with us as we erect a stone of remembrance and find ourselves encouraged in the presence of the same living God that all the generations before us found hope in.

The Encouragers Christian Writers Group

STONE TABLE

OPTICAL ILLUSIONS

by Rachel Critchley

"In the beginning God created the heavens and the earth"
(Genesis 1:1, NIV)

****

When I was growing up, a picture of a woman sitting in a garden was hanging in the family room. She was looking serenely toward a tree. That was a delightful picture to see but if you studied the picture, the face of Jesus would appear in the tree. When you looked past the obvious you observed additional information.

I have come to enjoy all kinds of optical illusions: the pictures that become another picture, the 3-D images which appear from a fuzzy haze and the blobs or dashes that become a picture or a word. All you have to do is concentrate. Look past the obvious and more will become apparent.

When I see a bird flying and chirping or providing for its young, I enjoy the beauty added to my environment. As I look past the obvious, I "see" all of the animals God put on earth in order to make my life better. One special animal in particular is my dog, Molly. She lightens my mood and puts a smile on my face every time I see her.

When I see a plow (or tractor) turning the soil to provide food for nourishment, I enjoy watching the food production process. God embedded our planet with metals so we would be able to make implements to plow the land. As I look past the obvious, I "see" all the various metals God put on earth in order to make my life better. One special metal to me is the one in my wedding ring.

My ring is a circular metal object with thirty years of cherished memories gently tied to it.

When I see a sunset, I enjoy the beauty of the changing colors displaying their nightly show for me. As I look past the obvious, I "see" God at work in nature all around me adding beauty to make my life better. My special area is nature itself. The outdoors is visual proof that God loves me, wants me to be happy and that He provides for my needs. God provides the cathedral of nature I enjoy.

I want to always look past the obvious and observe the limitless gifts God has given.

Prayer: "God, please open my eyes so I can see all that you have provided to make my life better. Amen."

Stepping Stones:

Look around your surroundings this week and try to see beyond the obvious. What do you see? How have your new eyes impacted you?

_____

_____

_____

_____

_____

_____

_____

_____

_____

_____

GOD'S BEAUTIFUL CREATION

by Stella Rome Carroll

In the beginning God created the heaven and the earth. And God called the dry land Earth; and the gathering together of the waters called He Seas: and God saw that it was good. (Genesis 1:1, 10 KJV)

****

Bible school would begin at 6:00 p.m. and I wanted to be ready. Our theme for the week was "God's Beautiful Creation." I quickly stopped by my house and grabbed the fish bowl that contained three gold fish. Placing the fish bowl in the center of the table with something beautiful in it that God created would be the right touch!

The children marveled at the gold fish. I gave them the opportunity to name the fish. Excitedly, they named the fish: Abraham, Moses, and Billy Graham. Our lesson taught that we were responsible for taking care of our beautiful world. The children loved the gold fish and listened intently to the lesson.

The next day I rushed into the room to discover that the gold fish were dead. Panicking, I grabbed up the bowl and went rushing down the hall to another room and hid the bowl up on a high shelf just before the children came skipping into our room. Naturally the children asked, "Where are Abraham, Moses and Billy Graham?" I simply said, "They're not here right now but they will be back tomorrow." They kept asking questions and I kept avoiding the truth.

The next day, I raced to Wal-Mart and described the size fish I needed. Uninterested, the clerk slapped the net into the tank and flipped it up, throwing the fish across the floor. She picked them up and bagged them. Irritated, I wanted to say something about what we were studying, but I was in such a hurry I held my tongue.

As the children streamed into the room, one of the children asked, "Is that really Abraham, Moses and Billy Graham?" Hands on her hips and a raised eyebrow indicated she didn't believe they were the same fish.

The next evening when I arrived, once again, the gold fish were dead. I hid the gold fish bowl on that same shelf and then went back to my room to sit down and pray. The children ran into the room and immediately asked, "Where are the fish?"

"Please sit down and listen carefully," I instructed. I explained what had happened and I told them about the clerk at Wal-Mart who did not care about God's beautiful world. I described how she had flung the fish onto the floor and how she did not keep the water clean in the tanks. They listened closely. I reminded them of our lesson, "God expects us to take care of His beautiful world." The children and I learned a valuable lesson that day about taking care of God's beautiful creation by hearing and speaking the truth!

Prayer: "Father, please remind me of the beauty of your truths. Amen"

Stepping Stones:

Have you ever been caught in a lie, even a well intentioned one? How did you react? Do you consider God's beautiful creation in your daily life? What parts of His creation are you thankful for?

AN UNSELFISH, SELFISH DECISION

by Pamela McCormick

And God said, "Let there be lights in the expanse of the heavens to separate the day from the night. And let them be for signs and for seasons, and for days and years, and let them be lights in the expanse of the heavens to give light upon the earth." And it was so.
(Genesis 1:14-15 ESV)

****

The night cried out in the darkness, "Where is the light of the starry sky?"

The starry sky replied, "When will the night go away?"

Neither the night nor the starry sky was satisfied.

The stars made a deal with the night. The night listened.

The stars wanted to be seen first by people, when they looked into the night sky.

The night agreed on one condition. The night asked, "Could the night drop the first letter in its name and change it to an "L?"

The stars said okay, but later realized that if night was instead light, why then would the stars be needed anymore?

As a result, the stars did not shine as bright, for they did not see their significance anymore. "What good are we, if we can't be seen?" asked the stars.

The night then replied, "You don't understand. You will be the light. See, I have been darkness and now by being light, you are helping me. I need you to shine bright, because the darkness is so black, and too much darkness is sad."

So the next time, you look into the sky and see all the stars, remember the night too, for it was when the night surrendered its darkness to the light of the stars above, it became more beautiful and bright. Because the night was willing to unselfishly give up its darkness, the moon came to call. The night became even brighter.

Did the night do this purposefully to help itself, without thought of the light it was gaining? All that's known are these words:

Then I said to myself, "Oh, he even sees me in the dark! At night I'm immersed in the light!" It's a fact: darkness isn't dark to you; night and day, darkness and light, they're all the same to you." Psalms 139:11-12 The Message

Darkness will remain darkness, until an open door welcomes the Light.

Prayer: "Holy Father, though the darkness surrounds me and desires to envelope me, You are always with me. Open my eyes, Father, and help me see that You love me too much to let me stay in the darkness, but desire instead that I would open the door and welcome the light. When I see just the darkness, I am missing what You are trying to teach me. I welcome Your Light. Illumine me, God, with Your Presence and speak peace to me and to others who struggle to see You. When I am afraid, I will trust in You, because even the darkness is not darkness to You. Amen."

Stepping Stones:

Do you struggle to see Jesus in your circumstances? Have you ever felt like the darkness was encompassing you and making you ineffective? Jesus Himself is the light of the world. How does He bring light to your world?

_____

_____

_____

_____

_____

_____

_____

_____

_____

_____

DISSATISFIED

by Cathy Biggerstaff

*And God saw everything that He had made, and behold, it was very good
and He approved it completely.
(Genesis 1:31 AMP)*

****

"I don't think I know you, young man," I said as I approached, ready to shake hands. I was greeting guests at my great granddaughter's first birthday party.

"My name is Everett," he said, his chin pointing up at me and his neck bent back in a strained position.

Bending toward him I asked, "How old are you, Everett?"

"I am three years old and I hate brown hair," he said pulling at a sprig of his hair.

His mother explained that he had been born blond but, as he aged, his hair was getting darker and darker. Some people in the family had made comments about it and Everett processed the remarks as being negative.

I got down on my knees in front of him and told him how amazing it is that he has brown hair. I told him that on the day he was made, God went to His workbench and said, "Hmmm, I am making Everett today and I am going to pick out just the right parts for him. I'll give him beautiful blue eyes to see the world through and soft brown hair that will start out light and get darker as he gets older. He'll get two arms made for hugging, two strong legs for running, and a brain with a brand new computer for thinking. Then two good ears so he can hear his mom's voice, a nose and a smiling mouth and Everett will be finished."

"Do you know what happened when God finished putting all the parts of you together?" I asked. Everett shook his head as I continued. "He looked at you and smiled and said, Ummm mmmmm! This is good." Then He picked you up and danced around the workshop with you saying over and over, "This is good. Everett is perfect. I love Everett just like He is."'"

Everett smiled and ran off to eat birthday cake. I had held his attention as long as a three year old will allow. I continued to move around the room, more heavy-hearted than before, knowing a three year old has a mindset of not measuring up because his hair is the wrong color.

Prayer: "Creator God, help me see myself today as you see me. Remind me often that you look at me and say, "It is good. I love you just like you are. No corrections needed. Amen."

Stepping Stones:

What does it mean to you to know that God looks at you and He sees beauty and perfection? Write a word of thanksgiving for creating you just the way you are. Acknowledge that His work is good.

_____

_____

_____

_____

_____

_____

_____

_____

_____

_____

_____

_____

_____

REMEMBER THE VAN

by Annette Gates

Pharaoh sent for Joseph at once, and he was quickly brought from the prison. After he shaved and changed his clothes, he went in and stood before Pharaoh. (Genesis 41:14 NLT)

****

Picture Joseph, languishing in prison for two long years, seemingly forgotten. Daily he goes about the same old prison routine. One day the Pharaoh sends for him and his life turns completely around. You never know when God is going to show up and solve your dilemma.

After my husband died, there was a van I didn't need anymore and really needed to sell. I tried everything I knew to try to get rid of it. Desperation and worry began to set in. I would never have expected to make a connection that led to the sale of the van while I was registering for lab work at the hospital's Outpatient Department. It was the last thing on my mind at the time.

As I was making small talk with the lady at the registration desk, the other lady sitting in the area behind the desk picked up on the statement I made about having a van I needed to sell. She said, "My husband knows a man who buys vehicles and fixes them up, let me put you in touch with him." I thanked her and exchanged contact information with her. Two days later, the van was sold and on a trailer being hauled away. God showed up to solve a problem when I wasn't even looking for Him to move on it.

Since then, when other issues pop into my thoughts and worry begins to crowd my mind, I hear a Heavenly voice saying, "Remember the van." Right away my mind can rest, knowing God's going to show up with a solution when I least expect it. If you're tempted to worry, "Remember the van." Your solution is on the way.

Prayer: "Thank you Father for showing us that you are working even when it doesn't look like it to us. Our best is always at the forefront of Your mind. Amen."

Stepping Stones:

What is causing you to worry today? Are you willing to be flexible as God directs your solution? He may answer your prayer in ways you aren't expecting. Has He done that for you before?

_____

_____

_____

_____

_____

_____

_____

_____

_____

_____

_____

_____

_____

May you continually grow in the grace and knowledge of our Lord and Savior Jesus Christ.
In His Love,
Lorna
Psalm 42:1

SHAKING IT UP

by Lorna Hawley

"Now go; I will help you speak and will teach you what to say." Exodus 4:12 (NIV)

****

How many times have you read these words: Shake Well before Using? Chances are, we have all experienced neglect in following this directive and ended up tasting a much diluted juice or getting just the oil when pouring dressing on our salad.

The purpose of "shaking well" is to receive the full benefit of the contents of the container, to taste the full flavor, to enjoy the product the way it was intended, to achieve the maximum results. Life is the same way, if we desire to follow God's directions.

Sometimes He has to shake us up for the purpose of being more effective for Him. We tend to get complacent and settle into a comfortable groove (rut) in our lives. We don't want to get out of our comfort zone. Our lives may be going along smoothly and we don't want things to change. Or our lives are in turmoil and we don't want to be shaken any more.

Often times His plan is far beyond our comprehension. We feel we are not equipped to do what He is calling us to do. We feel inadequate, fearful, timid. You are not alone. Moses, a mighty man of God, felt the same way. In Exodus 3:10 God told Moses that He was sending him to Pharaoh to deliver the children of Israel out of Egypt. Moses started making excuses, "Who am I that

I should go to Pharaoh? What would I say? I am not eloquent." At each objection, God patiently told Moses He would equip him. You see it wasn't about Moses, nor is it about us; it is all about God.

God desires to use us to do His Kingdom work. Just as He had to shake Moses up by getting his attention with the burning bush, so God will shake us up to get our attention and prepare us to accomplish His plan. The bigger the task, the greater the shaking may be so God can equip us and make us pliable, ready to do His will.

I don't like diluted juice or salad dressing. Likewise, God does not like diluted Christians. We need to be full strength and serve Him heartily. It is a good thing when we are shaken by God, for His purposes. The next time you feel that God is shaking you up, say, "Yes, God," and get ready to see Him do a great thing through you, to His Honor and Glory.

Prayer: "Dear Lord, please forgive me for becoming settled and complacent in my walk with You. Help me be submissive to your shaking and willing to be taken out of my comfort zone when You call me to serve you in unfamiliar areas. Help me remember that You will always equip me to do what You ask of me. Help me be faithful in serving you. Amen."

Stepping Stones:

How has God shaken your world, moving you out of your comfortable rut? What did you learn from the experience? Are you a diluted Christian or do you serve God with all your strength?

_____

_____

_____

_____

_____

_____

_____

_____

_____

_____

_____

_____

_____

_____

A NEW SONG OF VICTORY

by Mary Edwards

God is my strength, God is my song, and, yes! God is my salvation. This is the kind of God I have and I'm telling the world! Exodus 15:2 (The Message)

****

Fear and confusion kept me in hiding. My body struck by the ever so loving hand of a hung-over mother. Men touching me in ways and places I instinctively knew were wrong; a mere warm up before my Mom slept with them. Painful recollections, and unforgivable.

I turned my back, arms closed across my chest, and rejected all possibility of ever regaining respect for parents, men, authority, myself and God. My life's die was cast. I did exactly as satan wanted me to. I drank. I fell prey to abuse from myself and others. Suicide planning peppered my days. I sobbed in my pillow when I just couldn't look at myself in the mirror any longer. My life was ugly and so was the reflection I saw and wanted to spit on. I was tired of being hurt, mad, sad, disgusted, ashamed and angry at myself and God. Satan held me in his hands and was singing a victory chant over me.

I had to make a choice. My everyday life had to change. I crashed to the floor and cried out to God. I had to stop running from Him in anger and start moving toward Him. The intent of the evil one was to create distance between me and God. I had to intentionally return to Him and let Him embrace my hurting soul. I accepted in my heart that Jesus knows each painful memory and is aware of my feelings. He took it to the cross.

Each day I am filled with His Spirit and through that power, I am healing. Ugly is being replaced by the beauty of forgiveness. I know God is holding my hand and healing my inner child. The adult sees through God's eyes now. Papa God shares with me every good promise of healing and victory in Him as I embrace peace through His Son.

Healing came when I made a deliberate choice to put away things of the past and look forward. I continuously pray that God will help me find ways to set boundaries in my thinking: letting go of the past, forgiving myself and others, and moving forward in peace though Him. He is proud of the person I am becoming.

Prayer: "Heavenly Father, with all my heart, I praise you for saving this messed up person. There are so many victims of abuse in this world. Help them when they feel helpless. Love them when they don't feel any love at all. Thank you for being patient. In Jesus Name, Amen."

Stepping Stones:

Is the child in you feeling rejection? Are you holding on to bitter hurt? You no longer have to accept satan's abuse. No need to keep feeling trapped and empty when you can be free and filled with Him. Make a decision today to turn away from the chants of the evil one and learn the song of victory Jesus wants to teach you. What would you like to give to Jesus today?

_____

_____

_____

_____

_____

_____

_____

_____

_____

_____

_____

STRENGTH FOR THE MOMENT

by Cathy Biggerstaff

The LORD is my strength and my song, and he has become my salvation;
this is my God, and I will praise him, my father's God, and I will exalt him. (Exodus 15:2 ESV)

****

It had been five years. I thought I had shed all the tears, run the gamut of emotions and made peace with God in my heart. This Easter season was proving me wrong. I knew without looking at the calendar what day it was: the anniversary of our first-born's death. Stacie was born with a heart defect and struggled to live a day. Her April birthday generally falls within the Easter season.

This year, as emotions pulled me back five years, it felt like I was experiencing her death all over again. Our pastor was doing a Lenten series on people at the cross, taking one person per week and looking at the crucifixion from their point of view. This Sunday morning the person was Mary, the mother of Jesus.

I ached for Mary as she looked on while the riotous crowd chose to set the criminal Barabbas free. She had to know what the consequences of their decision meant for her son. She followed Him along the Via Dolorosa as He dragged Himself up the hill, stumbling from weakness and loss of blood. She was part of the crowd watching at the cross as He slowly died. There isn't any mention of her weeping during any of this. She exhibited strength in the midst of excruciating difficulty, possibly willing that strength to help her son through this, as mothers sometimes do.

There I sat on that April morning, on a weathered pew, immersed in Mary's world. I ran through the similarities and differences in us and our situations. At least my child didn't have to suffer like yours did; I spoke in my heart to Mary. I thanked God for sparing me that and for knowing me well enough to know I couldn't have survived it. Still, I coveted Mary's strength. I wanted it for myself.

And then I heard God's voice speak into my soul, "Cathy, I don't play favorites. The same strength I gave to Mary, I gave to you." My spirit immediately lifted as I wrapped my mind around the fact that God loves me the same way He loves Mary. And He has placed within me the strength I need to weather any storm. I left church that day buoyed with a new resolve, a strength I didn't know I already possessed, and an appreciation for how God uses people in the Bible to speak to present day needs.

Prayer: "Heavenly Father, just as Moses and his people sang to you, You are my strength and my song, I will praise and exalt You. Amen."

Stepping Stones:

What characters in the Bible have taught you something about living life today? Praise God today for including that account in the Bible, just for you.

_____

_____

_____

_____

_____

_____

_____

_____

_____

_____

THE CURIO CABINET

by Lorna Hawley

He put the lampstand in the tent of meeting, opposite the table on the south side of the tabernacle, and set up the lamps before the LORD, as the LORD had commanded Moses.(Exodus 40:24-25 NASB)

****

Is there a lighted curio cabinet in your home? What is its' purpose? If you are like me, you keep special treasures in your cabinet, things that I want to showcase, things that I really like and want to protect and keep on display for all to see.

I like to think of my life as a lighted cabinet. What am I displaying in my showcase? Am I letting the light of Jesus shine, or are people seeing behavior displayed in me that does not honor Christ nor showcase a Christ-like attitude to others. Just as the lights in my curio cabinet clearly display my treasures, my life should be illuminated by the light of Jesus.

Sometimes the lights in my display cases show up imperfections in a piece. I want to polish it, mend any cracks, turn the damaged area to the back, or somehow make the piece look beautiful for those who gaze on it. I am one of those damaged, imperfect pieces in God's showcase. God didn't just mask my flaws; He made me into a new creature. He made me beautiful again through Jesus. Therefore, I want to display His light in the best possible way to all those around me.

I think of my life, not only as a lighted showcase, but also as a museum. People are always watching, observing, and studying. I never know when something they see in me will have an impact on them. Just as some people only go to a museum once, people may only cross my path once. I need to let my light shine all the time. Other people will make several visits to a museum and study certain pieces in depth, just as some people will enter my life at different intervals and stay for differing amounts of time. For those visits, consistency will be the key so that whenever I am observed, people will see the same steadfast light of Jesus shining through.

It's all about the light! I keep a bright clean bulb in my curio cabinet highlighting my treasures, so they will be seen at their best. My life should be lived so that my Christian light shines brightly to the world around me, that they may see God and desire a personal relationship with Him. We never know who is looking at our treasures.

"Let your light so shine before men, that they may see your good works and glorify your Father which is in heaven."
(Matthew 5:16 KJV)

Prayer: "Lord, please help me to consistently shine brightly for You. Amen."

Stepping Stones:

What things in your life do you consider treasures? If you were a curio cabinet what would people see displayed there? Does your light shine the way you want it to? What changes can you make to shine brighter so all the world can see Jesus in you?

_____

_____

_____

_____

_____

_____

_____

_____

_____

_____

_____

_____

MY ONE TRUE OBSESSION

by Cathy Biggerstaff

When Moses came down from Mount Sinai, with the two tablets of the testimony in his hand as he came down from the mountain, Moses did not know that the skin of his face shone because he had been talking with God. (Exodus 34:29 ESV)

****

One of the prayer requests that day at Bible study was, "that Jesus would be our One True Obsession." One True Obsession sounds like a great name for a perfume, I thought while others continued praying. I immediately pictured an ornate, crystal bottle with a long, gold tasseled bulb. It was sitting on an oval crystal tray, along with a hairbrush and a mirror whose handles were gold, real gold: gold through and through, not a coating of gold, or painted to look like gold.

Later in the day my thoughts connected with a memory from the distant past. At that time, our church felt a desperate need to pray for God to send some younger families with children to fill our pews. We agreed that anyone who wanted to participate would come to the church early in the morning on Tuesdays before we went our separate ways to work and school or other activities.

As I was leaving one of those prayer sessions a friend and I hugged and wished each other a good day. As the day progressed I noticed that every time there was the slightest breeze or flutter of air movement, I smelled my friend's perfume, reminding me of the prayer we'd shared that morning.

In the verses I've quoted above, Moses was changed by being in God's presence on the mountain. Moses had begged God to let him see His face. Other verses in Exodus tell us that if anyone sees God's face they will die. Moses had favor with God so God offered a compromise to Moses' request. God placed Moses in the cleft of a rock and shielded his view while He passed by. Then He called to Moses and allowed Moses to see His back. The glory of God shined on Moses and, even forty days later when he came down off the mountain, his face was beaming brightly. Moses' face shone so brightly that people had to block their eyes or look away. It was evidence to the people in the camp that Moses had, indeed, been in the presence of the Holy God of Israel.

When you start your day with God in prayer, the fragrance of God will follow you throughout the day. You will be changed by being in His presence. As we meet each day, with all its blessings and challenges, let's put on our One True Obsession as a witness to those around us.

Prayer: "Heavenly Father, you are our one true obsession. Accompany us through this day from start to finish and let us witness to your goodness and mercy as we share your fragrance with others. Amen."

Stepping Stones:

What is your one true obsession? What causes you to remember Jesus and take Him with you through each day? Can people see a difference in you after you've spent time with Him? Do you carry His fragrance with you throughout the day?

_____

_____

_____

_____

_____

_____

_____

_____

_____

_____

_____

_____

_____

MUMBLERS AND GRUMBLERS

by Cathy Biggerstaff

And the people complained in the hearing of the LORD about their misfortunes, and when the LORD heard it, his anger was kindled, and the fire of the LORD burned among them and consumed some outlying parts of the camp. (Numbers 11:1 ESV)

****

I hit the button to turn off the annoyance of the alarm and jumped out of bed, late again from hitting the snooze button one too many times. Dancing from one foot to the other on the frigid floor, I mumbled as I made the bed. In the bathroom, I found there was no hot water. I was the last family member to bathe that morning and the others had used up all the hot water. I grumbled about the rudeness of the people I live with and the size of the water heater. Dressing, one shoe of the only pair of shoes that matched my outfit was missing. I yelled into the universe, "Why do these things always happen to me when I'm in a hurry?" No answer came. The rest of the morning fell into this same pattern as one thing after another didn't go my way. And I muttered under my breath and grumbled all the way to work.

As I drove my negativity to work, God reminded me of other people who mumbled and grumbled. God had rescued the Israelites from slavery in Egypt in a miraculous demonstration of His power. Now they were wandering in a desert with the Promise Land as their destination. God fed them every day, providing water to drink, clothes and shoes that never wore out, and made His presence visible to them.

Still, they grumbled and whined. They were tired of eating the same food day in and day out. God added quail to their daily diet, dropping it from the sky; all provided free of charge. Still they grumbled. Finally at the end of His patience, He decreed that none of the present generation wandering in the desert would enter the Promise Land.

I was mindful of the seriousness of mumbling and grumbling instead of being thankful for the blessings God has provided. As I revisited the blessings I woke up with that morning – a comfortable bed in a warm home with modern plumbing, clothes and shoes, food for breakfast, a job to provide for my family's needs and a car to get me there – I was ashamed of my negative attitude. Tears filled my eyes as I repented, asking God to forgive me. Now when I find myself falling back into my old negative ways, I look in the mirror and repeat, "The mumblers and grumblers didn't make it to the Promise Land."

Prayer: "Father, you have blessed me abundantly out of your great storehouse. Remove any negative thoughts I might have and replace them with joy and thanksgiving as I serve you each day. Thank you, Lord, for always providing my daily bread. Amen."

Stepping Stones:

Are you guilty of mumbling and grumbling instead of recognizing your blessings? Write God a letter thanking Him for your blessings and repenting of your negative attitude when things don't go your way.

_____

_____

_____

_____

_____

_____

_____

_____

_____

_____

_____

_____

_____

SCARED STRAIGHT INTO HIS ARMS

by Mary Jane Downs

*The eternal God is your refuge, and underneath are the everlasting arms.
(Deuteronomy 33:27 NIV)*

****

Oh, what a beautiful snow it was. The extra large flakes falling were exciting because I had been praying to see some snow this year. However, along with the beauty came the mess. Salt-water slush had dried all over my car. I knew I would need to get it washed quickly.

So, Monday morning, Buddy (my dog) and I went to get the car washed along with the some other errands I needed to run. When I go places, I love to take Buddy. His joyful expression as he hangs his head out the window is priceless. Pulling into the car wash, I inserted my money and made my wash and rinse selections. All was well until I pulled into the washing bay.

As the machines moved over the car, Buddy began to cower and then slither into the front seat beside me. He was shaking uncontrollably while trying to stay close to me. Buddy instinctively knew, if he could get into the arms of his master, he would be protected and comforted.

I talked to him softly as I stroked his head. I told him how brave he was, that he would be fine and it would be over soon. Buddy may not have understood the words I spoke but he could understand my tone and intent. As we left the car wash, Buddy was timid bur he rewarded me with many licks of thanks. By the time I drove to the street, he was in the back seat, his tail wagging, and ready for the window to be opened again.

In that moment, I realized Buddy and I are alike in how we react to our fears. When I am overcome with fear, I also instinctively get into my Master's arms for comfort and strength. God speaks words of encouragement to my spirit, sometimes through His Word and sometimes through people around me. The softness of His voice helps me focus on His power to get me through. When I sense that the danger is over, I sit up, straighten my clothes, and thank God he was there to embrace me. As I relax, I resume the activities I was working on before the crisis began.

What do you do when fear comes? Learning to run into the arms of your heavenly Father takes time but it is worth the effort. If you are not sure how to begin, take a lesson from Buddy; spend time at the feet of your master, listen to your master's comforting words and learn to respond to your master's comfort with thanks. With a little practice you will instinctively get into the arms of our Heavenly Father in times of uncertainty.

Prayer: "Teach me to run into your arms when fear wants to invade my mind. You are my comforter and friend. Amen"

Stepping Stones:

What scares you? What do you do when you're afraid? How does God fit into your response to fear? The phrase, "Do not fear," appears 365 times in the Bible. That's one for every day of the year! God knew we were going to be afraid sometimes, but He doesn't want us to be. Thank Him for the ways He has kept you from fear.

_____

_____

_____

_____

_____

_____

_____

_____

_____

_____

_____

_____

_____

WHEREVER I GO

by Stella Rome Carroll

Be strong and of good courage; be not afraid, neither be thou dismayed: for the Lord thy God is with thee whithersoever thou goest.

(Joshua 1:9 KJV)

****

Each one of us faces changes at one time or another in our life time. It is how we respond to those changes that reflects who we are and in whom we believe. An opportunity for change actually fell at my feet before I was ready.

A few months ago, I was hospitalized twice. I was flat on my back for seven days each time. Due to back surgery years earlier, I had been left numb from the waist down so I was already restricted to a wheel chair. After these latest hospitalizations, I lost all my strength and was sent to a nursing home for rehab. Because I could not stand at all, a lift was used to get me out of bed and into a chair. After two weeks of rehab I began to regain some of my strength, but not enough to go home.

My two sons and I researched assisted living homes only to find that the costs were exorbitant and I did not qualify for government help. Everywhere we turned I was told that I was in a pickle and I needed to weigh my options. "It sounds as if I have don't have any options," I responded to their pitying half- smiles.

My sons and I finally agreed on one of the least expensive homes but my money didn't stretch far enough. My sons held

37

several yard sales to sell my belongings and what they didn't sell was taken to Goodwill. My house was put on the market.

Friends asked me, "How are you taking losing everything?" I was surprised by their question. "It's just stuff," I responded. I was more disturbed about giving up the Sunday School class I was teaching than the absence of personal belongings. I dearly loved teaching my class and I felt it was my calling to teach God's Word.

Not long after adjusting to nursing home life, I began to sense that God was not through with me. There were residents living here with needs much greater than mine. I began talking to them and listening to them. These people are not just shriveled up bodies. They are people with great pasts, good hearts and are rich in what they can still give to others. God has enabled me to be an encourager and maybe, in a sense, still a teacher.

Prayer: "Dear Father, thank you for being with me wherever I go and for still using me for your purpose no matter where I find myself living. You are an amazing God who fills my life with wonderful blessings. Amen."

Stepping Stones:

Because of His great love for us, we don't have to be afraid when our circumstances are overwhelming. When have changes affected your life? How did God encourage you?

_____

_____

_____

_____

_____

_____

_____

_____

_____

_____

_____

_____

_____

_____

ARE YOU A BOAT?

by Lorna Hawley

David came to Saul and entered his service. Saul liked him very much, and David became one of his armor-bearers. (I Samuel 16:21 NIV)

****

Did you ever play the childhood game where you had to describe yourself in a category suggested by another child? It went like this, "What dog would you be if you had to be a dog." For a few moments think about what kind of boat you'd be if you had to be a boat.

Rowboat: "I can do it myself. I will decide where I want to go and I will get myself there. I don't need any help."

Hi-powered speed boat: "I am strong and powerful, flashy, better than the other boats. I am invincible."

Sail boat: "I am serene and peaceful, even though I live at the mercy of the wind, being sent to and fro with no power to keep a steady course?

Cruise ship: "I am impressive, exuding fun and adventure; calling you to leave the world behind and just party and play. I am looking for the good life with no responsibilities."

Did you find yourself in any of these examples? Consider one more boat.

Tug boat: "There's nothing fast or flashy about me, but I am dependable and steady, a team player. I gently, but firmly, maneuver larger vessels in and out of harbors. Sometimes smaller boats need me to come to their aide."

The tug boat's sole job is to serve other ships and boats. Without them, a commercial harbor could not function. The tug boat exemplifies greatness. It does not flaunt itself, nor draw attention to itself. It is not deterred from its' mission. Its moves are deliberate and with purpose. It guides consistently, firmly and correctly. It is always ready to give assistance.

That is how I picture the Christian life. We should not be seeking self recognition. We should be steadfast in the work that God has called us to; moving with deliberate and consistent purpose and direction, aiding our fellow Christians who are learning, struggling, need encouragement, or just desire fellowship. Just as a tug boat brings large ships safely into harbor, we as Christians should be instrumental in bringing people into the safe harbor of Jesus Christ.

Do you want to be seen as great in the eyes of the Lord? Be a tug boat, serving Him and others He has placed along your path.

Prayer: "Dear Lord, please help me never see anything you ask of me as menial, but to see it as an opportunity to serve. Help me faithfully follow your example of greatness by serving You and serving others. Amen."

Stepping Stones:

How would you define greatness? Which boat best describes you? What changes do you need to make in your life and beliefs to come closer to what God considers greatness to be?

_____

_____

_____

_____

_____

_____

_____

_____

_____

_____

_____

_____

_____

_____

THE BATTLE IS OVER

by Cathy Biggerstaff

"...the Lord saves not with sword and spear. For the battle is the Lord's, and he will give you into our hand." (I Samuel 17:47 ESV)

****

My husband and I spent a recent weekend with men and women who served in the 26th Infantry Division in Vietnam and other war theaters. It was an amazing experience for me to hear their stories. Most were in their teens when they volunteered or were drafted. They came from small towns where there was very little violence and within days after entering the Army, they found themselves in a foreign jungle being shot at by snipers. One man recounted that he was shot at on his first day in Vietnam.

They were a room full of wounded warriors, some physically, some mentally, but all changed for life. Their minds were full of unanswerable questions: "Was my sacrifice worth what it cost me and my family?" "Was it worth the loss of American lives?" "Did we do any good by being there?" One soldier consoled himself with the fact that the military had enhanced the infrastructure of the countries by building roads, bridges and other structures that remained when they left. It was little consolation, but the only good he could muster up in his mind.

Twice, through divine intervention, I have been linked to soldiers who were serving in battle, one in Afghanistan and one in Iraq. One was texting someone else and got me instead. I don't know how the other one got connected to me. After we established a rapport, I told them I was a warrior as well, a prayer warrior. I was able to witness to both of these men about the saving grace of Jesus. Neither one of them made a profession of faith while we were talking so I won't know until I get to Heaven if I made a difference in their lives. I have to leave that question unanswered for a while but I am satisfied knowing that, as a warrior, I did what was called for at the time. The rest is up to God.

In this life we are all engaged in a battle of one sort or another: the battle over good and evil, the battle over life and death, the battle over good choices and bad. Christians are blessed to be fighting from a position of victory because Christ paid the price and won the battle for us. It's time for all warriors to come home from the battlefield. Jesus is waiting with open arms to welcome us home.

Prayer: "Dearest Lord and Savior, thank you for paying the price and winning the wars we try to battle on our own. Urge us to come home to you, our Prince of Peace, Mighty God, Everlasting Father, and Wonderful Counselor. In you we find everything we need. Amen."

Stepping Stones:

Is there a battle raging in your heart? Give it to Jesus. The war is over and the battle has been won on the cross. Thank Him for paying the debt you owed but could not pay. When you see a veteran, thank him/her for their service and fighting for your freedom. Take time this week to send a card of thanks to your nearest VA Medical Center.

_____

_____

_____

_____

_____

_____

_____

_____

_____

_____

_____

HIS VOICE

by Stella Rome Carroll

And, behold, there came a voice unto him.
(1Kings 19:1 KJV)

****

For the past two months, a feeling of urgency kept pushing me to see a friend from high school, someone I hadn't seen in over forty years. She had lived on a street parallel to the street where I lived when we were young teens. Every morning, sunshine or rain, we shared the same bus stop and bus ride to school. While waiting, we spent our time talking about the things that had happened at school the day before.

After graduating from high school, we went in different directions. I had no clue as to where she now lived or how to contact her, yet I felt as if God was telling me to find her. I soon discovered someone who had a connection with Christina. She told me that health problems had put her in an assisted living home. I quizzed her as to which one and in what town but still could not get enough information to find her.

Two or three weeks later I was told she was in the hospital and she may have to have a foot amputated. Immediately, I called my nephew to accompany me the next morning to make the trip to visit her.

Just before we left, I decided to call the hospital to get her room number. I was told that she was not a patient there. I made a few calls to find the facility she had been transferred to. While waiting on a response, we got in the car and headed in that general direction. It wasn't long before I had the information we needed!

After a couple of wrong turns, we finally arrived at our destination. The center looked very welcoming and we soon found her room. She was asleep and I hesitated about entering her room but that urgent feeling overwhelmed me in that moment so I rolled my wheel chair into the room and parked myself next to her bed. In a soft voice, I said, "Christina."

She woke up and I told her who I was. She lit up like a Christmas tree. The joy on her face gave me such a blessing that I knew God had brought me to this very moment. We both talked as if we only had five minutes to cover forty years. Sadly, a few weeks later the infection affected her heart and she passed away. I was so glad I had listened to His voice and took action by following His lead.

Prayer: "Dear Father, I pray that I will always be receptive to your voice. Thank you for the ways you speak into my life giving me opportunities to serve you and others. Amen."

Stepping Stones:

When God speaks to you, how do you respond? Do you always follow His lead without hesitation? Are there times you are too busy to hear His voice? What can you do this week to clean out your ears so you can hear Him clearer?

_____

_____

_____

_____

_____

_____

_____

_____

_____

_____

_____

_____

_____

_____

UNEXPECTED JOY

by Carolyn Wease

The joy of the Lord is your strength.
(Nehemiah 8:10 ESV)

****

Six years after the birth of my second child by Cesarean Section, I found myself pregnant for the third time. All went well, aside from the nearly 60 pounds I had gained. With my first delivery, God filled my mind with a gospel song which gave me peace. He gave me a scripture for comfort during my second operation. A few weeks before my delivery date, I asked God to give me a song or a scripture to help me overcome my anxious feeling as He'd done before.

When the day of my Cesarean arrived, my peace had not come. After being prepped for surgery, the nurse left my side for a moment. I was asking God once more to give me something to ease my fears when the nurse returned and we were out the door and rolling down the hall. Suddenly, I realized I wasn't afraid anymore. I was lighthearted and giddy, feeling like I didn't have a care in the world. Total peace and pure joy overcame me. I was even laughing and joking with the doctors. Beautiful baby girl number three arrived on schedule and within a couple of days we were out of the hospital and back at home.

A few weeks later I was doing some light housework when I realized that God never gave me a song or scripture to take with me into the operating room. Before there was time to ponder this, the words *the joy of the Lord is your strength* rang in my heart. All of a sudden the scope of what God had done was clear to me. He had answered my prayer, but he had done it in an unexpected way. He wanted me to experience an unforgettable lesson. He let me feel the impact of the scripture.

The joy and lighthearted feeling I experienced was God's answer to my prayer. The joy overcame all fear and gave me the strength to accomplish my task. The strength I gained through that joy was far above any I had known before. Through this fearful time, God showed me that His Word is more than just words printed in black ink on white paper. His Word is alive. It is because of that life we can believe and be set free from fear in any circumstance. Though all else may fail, God's WORD will never fail.

Prayer: "Thank you for your mighty works in my life, Lord. You fill me with your joy and give me strength. Your Word is alive and available when I ask. Amen."

Stepping Stones:

As you pray this week, ask God to reveal His living Word to you in ways He never has before. What did He show you? What scriptures did He impress on you?

_____

_____

_____

_____

_____

_____

_____

_____

_____

_____

_____

_____

_____

OUT OF WEAKNESS, A WITNESS

by Mary Jane Downs

I know that you can do all things; no purpose of yours can be thwarted.
(Job 42:2 NIV)

✱✱✱✱

My lifelong battle with ADHD and memory issues caused me to experience great stress and anxiety. As a youngster, I knew there was something different about me. Even though I wanted to please my parents and teachers, the learning to learn and to read and write was more of a struggle than I could handle. My brain would not function in ways that would cause me to recall what I needed to remember. I felt stupid, especially when I saw looks of disappointment, and became introverted and my self-esteem remained low.

In my twenties, I married. John loved to read. I kept observing his passion for the written word. As John shared details of a book, I began to realize I was missing out by refusing to read. I made a decision and then pushed through my fears to read a book for pleasure: "Blue Camilla" by Frances Parkinson Keyes. I became so engrossed in the story that when I finished, I was left wanting more. That one book gave me a new beginning.

In my thirties, my husband died of heart disease. As I followed God's guidance through my difficult times, wisdom developed. My desire to help others also sparked a desire to write.

In my forties, I shared short little notes as the opportunity arose. I thought that was all God would require. It felt safe. However, He envisioned my writing reaching a much broader audience. As God revealed his desire, I was enthusiastic at first. Then fear filtered through and I became afraid of failure. I was paralyzed by the "what if'" questions and the "I can't" thoughts, but my fears did not hinder God one bit. He gently encouraged me to learn so I could conqueror those fears and fulfill my destiny.

Finally, in my middle fifties, my fears melted and I moved forward. I acknowledged I would no longer be in control of my writing gift. Ultimately, 1 told God that if he would inspire the words, then I would be His willing vessel.

Isn't that just like God to take our greatest weakness and fears and turn them into our greatest strength to witness for Him. We may not get on board right away with God's vision, but that does not offend or deter Him. God remains steadfast in mentoring us until we can see and claim the victory for ourselves.

Prayer: "Lord, thank you for leading me and showing me Your will. Develop Your courage within me so I can step out and do Your perfect will in my life. Amen."

Stepping Stones:

Have you ever felt different than the people around you? Has God called you to do something that takes you out of your comfort zone? How has He worked in your life to bring strength out of your weakness?

BEAUTY AMID THE WEEDS

by Pamela McCormick

"The Lord is my rock, my fortress and my deliverer; my God is my rock, in whom I take refuge. He is my shield and the horn of my salvation, my stronghold." Psalms 18:2 (NIV)

****

"Bloom where you are planted."

"But God, You don't understand."

"Bloom where you are planted."

A perfectly manicured garden speaks to my soul. It requires the commitment of an avid gardener who has the desire, knowledge and resources to keep the garden looking beautiful. Without that, weeds will sprout and try their best to choke out the developing plants. Ever wonder why God created weeds?

Life isn't always easy. Pulling weeds out of the ground can be like digging up our own roots, our beginnings. Sometimes we would rather avoid the times that were hard to understand in the past. Just like the weeds in the garden, we question why they happened, but the things we can't control are all part of making us who we are and who we will be. Those weeds can be responsible for where we end up when we say goodbye to this life and go home.

Once the weeds take hold and take over, the only remedy is to start over by plowing up the garden space. We are being turned like plowed soil, so we can become the rich soil needed to produce hope for others. Many are struggling with the same weeds of despair and heartache that we do. They can't see all that God has prepared for those who will love and trust Him. Having been through it ourselves, we can be advocates for others; an example of what God can and will do for them.

The weeds represent the struggles that bring us to our knees and help us see our need for God. God takes our chaos and brings us to the realization that we need Him if we are going to make it. Weeds will rise up and threaten to destroy us or they will make us stronger, knowing there is a purpose, and it's God given.

I believe God gave us weeds so we could understand that ugliness will happen in life. We won't like it, but He guarantees He will be right there beside us, giving us the ability to keep growing. Will you bloom where you are planted?

Prayer: "God, I hear You say, "Bloom where you are planted." Thank You for enabling me. You are my hope when life is hard. Thank You, that You use the dark as well as the light to grow me into the woman You want me to be. Here is my life, Lord. Take it and grow something beautiful in me. Amen."

Stepping Stones:

Are there weeds threatening to overtake the garden of your heart? What growing experiences make you an advocate for others during their struggles? Thank God today for being an expert gardener, pruning and weeding you to make you the beautiful servant He needs.

_____

_____

_____

_____

_____

_____

_____

_____

_____

_____

_____

_____

_____

HOW CAN THIS CHAOS BE PERFECTION?

by Annette Gates

As for God, His way is perfect. All the Lord's promises are true.
(Psalm 18:30a NLT).

****

The future King of Israel, David, made this declaration as he was being pursued by the current king and his armies. Under God's direction, David had been anointed the new king by the prophet Samuel. David had a sure promise from God. All the threatening and pursuit by the reigning king must have screamed the opposite to him. How could he make this proclamation? He remembered God's past actions in his own life and the testimonies from God's word and the nation's history. God's character overwhelmed David's circumstances and David knew he could depend on God to be faithful, to defend him and make His promises come true.

Imagine being in his place. For some that may not be too difficult. For two years now it hasn't been much of a stretch of the imagination for me. I suddenly and unexpectedly became a widow. I felt like I was abandoned in a dark wilderness, no light, no help, and no direction. We had started our journey in life together thirty eight years before with a commitment to God and each other. We had a plan: to have a home and family where God was first and to serve Him together wherever He led us. Yes, we had some ups and downs but God was always with us. We had raised two daughters who love the Lord and have three grandchildren who love Him too. We were all set for the next stage of our mission together, then all of a sudden my partner was gone, our plan was aborted. My heart was crying, "What now God?"

I couldn't see a future. Like David, I had to look to God's past provision and trust in His word that declares He has a plan and purpose for me. (Jeremiah 29:11) No, I don't know what it is yet, but knowing it is perfect keeps me coming back to God to walk me through each day. When the time is right He will show me the next step in His plan for me.

If you are in a desperate place, you have my prayers. If not, remember these words should you find yourself there. If you will replay in your mind the goodness and faithfulness of God, soon that truth will sink deeply into your spirit. You'll have the peace, hope and strength to make a declaration like David's.

Prayer: "Today I pray for those reading these words, precious Father. Please help them remember the things that will encourage and preserve them. If they need new experiences, show them your actions in life today. Freshly speak your promises to them through someone's words. Thank you, for you are always faithful. You love us with your eternal love that is so deep it cannot be measured. Amen."

Stepping Stones:

When has God's faithfulness been made real to you? What do you need today that only God can supply? What scripture verses have been precious to you in times of trouble?

_____

_____

_____

_____

_____

_____

_____

_____

_____

_____

_____

_____

_____

_____

ALPHABET OF GRACE

by Rachel Critchley

Some trust in chariots and some in horses,
but we trust in the name of the Lord our God. (Psalm 20:7 NIV)

****

All that You have given me

Because I am Your child

Can only be described as

Divine Grace.

Everyday, everywhere I constantly

Find myself in amazement of You my

God.

How do I qualify for this

Incredible gift of

Jesus — dying for my sins?

Keeping Your commandments (as best I can).

Letting others see me as a positive representation of You.

Making the most of the gifts you have given me.

Notice the small things and be respectful of all.

Omit temptation wherever it hides.

Pray for others and myself.

Quarrel less—listen more.

Read your book and study and learn.

Strive to be positive as life goes by.

Try to do my best each and every single day.

Use my gifts to reflect positively upon You.

Verses in the Bible are pathways to follow.

Wait—the gift I received—I will never deserve.

X, the unknown—what to do?

Yet I qualify because of Your Grace.

Zion—my home.

Prayer: "Lord, I am humbled at everything You have given me. The opportunities You make available and the love You have placed in my life never cease to amaze me. I am appreciative of the abundance You so generously provide. Amen"

Stepping Stones:

Make a list of some of the things Jesus has given you. How do you show your appreciation? Are you looking forward to your Heavenly home? What do you think you'll see there?

_____

_____

_____

_____

_____

_____

_____

_____

_____

_____

NO BATTERIES NEEDED

by Lorna Hawley

"Yea, though I walk through the valley of the shadow of death, I will fear no evil: for thou art with me; thy rod and thy staff they comfort me."
(Psalm 23:4 KJV)

****

As a child I was fascinated with my shadow. My friends and I tried different angles so we could grow bigger and bigger. As we mature though, shadows take on a new meaning for us. The meaning generally suggests something fearful. Do you feel like you are living in a huge shadow or trial? Does it seem like all you can see is the grey darkness of shadows? The thing about shadows is that they seem very real, because we can see them, but they actually have no substance.

In order to have a shadow, there must be light present. It is so easy to be focused on the shadow or trial, when that is where we are living. Take time to look beyond the edges of the shadow and notice the bright light.

Yes, we will have times when life is rough and we may even feel that we cannot survive a particular trial, but, as the Psalmist David wrote, we don't have to go through these valleys, these tough times, alone. We don't need to fear. The shadow is evidence of God's presence, for His shining light is there to guide us THROUGH the valley. We don't have to stay there if we are willing to walk with God and let His light lead us out of the valley.

Along with His light is His protection. The shepherd's rod is to keep predators away, and his staff is to keep us secure and close to Him. Psalm Twenty-three is talking about sheep and a shepherd. Jesus is our Good Shepherd and those who love Him are the sheep. Just as the real sheep are protected and made to feel secure by the shepherd when they stay close, so we can feel protected and secure when we stay close to Jesus, our shepherd.

Even when the shadows come, and especially when they come, Jesus is right there shining His light brightly for us, to show us the way to go. We don't have to live in the shadows of the past, what ifs, mistakes, hurts, frustrations, disappointments, or regrets. We are to walk through the valleys, not get bogged down there. Jesus desires for us to live and walk in His light. His light is eternal and constant. No batteries or electrical connections are ever needed.

Prayer: "Dear Jesus, forgive me when I get ensnared by the shadows. Help me look beyond it and see your light. Help me walk in your light as you walk with me through the valleys and shadows when they come. Amen."

Stepping Stones:

What shadows from past disappointments are keeping you from experiencing all that God has for you? Are you living in a rut? What can you do this week to step out of your comfortable place and change your present and your future?

WHO NEEDS A THEME PARK?

by Annette Gates

My heart has heard you say, "Come and talk with me."
And my heart responds. "Lord I am coming."
Psalm 27:8 (NLT)

****

Can you believe it? God wants to take a stroll with you!

Stop a moment and consider God's purpose in creating humankind: He wants our company. Recall the account from the book of Genesis describing God coming to walk with his people in the garden in the cool of the evening. Switch on your imagination and picture it; a garden so beautiful, it's beyond anything we can imagine, it defies description. It's a cool, peaceful evening and all work for the day has ceased. Suddenly you realize you're not alone. God himself, the creator of all that is, awakens your senses to His presence because He just wants to walk and talk with the ones He loves.

Centuries later David, the King of Israel, is hearing God say, "Talk with me." Centuries beyond that, God's heart of love hasn't changed and it never will. He is still calling to the hearts of mankind, "Come, sit and talk with me."

Won't you bless God's heart today? Tell Him, "I am coming." Shut out the noise of this world and let Him transport you to a peaceful place with Him. He can create that place wherever we are when I say "Lord I am coming."

Prayer: "Precious Father, You're calling us to you, please soften our hearts and still our minds so that we will hear you and say, "Lord I am coming." Thank you for your heart of love, your desire to be with us. Thank you for the blessings you're waiting to pour out on us. Thank you for making your words to us so sweet that we hang on every one and always hunger for more of you. Amen."

Stepping Stones:

Where do you meet with Jesus to sit and talk each day? One lady has placed two chairs in the room where she has her quiet time. As she passes by, it reminds her that Jesus is waiting for her to "come and sit" with Him. What do you do to encourage yourself to spend time with Him each day?

_____

_____

_____

_____

_____

_____

_____

_____

_____

_____

_____

_____

WHERE ARE WE GOING?

by Stella Rome Carroll

I will instruct you and teach you in the way that you should go; I will counsel you with my loving eye on you. (Psalm 32:8 NIV)

****

The minute we climbed into my car, my six year old foster child asked, "Where are we going?" Over and over, he would ask without let up. To be perfectly honest, it drove me nuts. After a full day of stress at work, I felt like getting in the car and just driving, somewhere, anywhere. I didn't even want to think about where I was going.

Because of the day I had endured at the office, I wasn't ready to face helping with homework just yet and I sure wasn't ready to mediate any squabbles between my son and my foster son. I needed to wind down before I would be prepared to tackle any other frustrations. After hearing one thousand times, "Where are we going?" I would tell him anything to calm him down, even if I ended up just driving around the block.

A few days later, I was reading an informative article in a Foster Parent newsletter. It explained why a large percentage of foster kids always want to know, "Where are we going?" The author stated that most foster children didn't understand why they had been jerked out of their homes. Some had even been moved from one foster home to another causing them to have a real fear of it happening to them again. They were afraid of the unknown. They had a need to feel secure.

Ashamed of my actions, tears flowed down my face. I loved my foster son and I did not want him to be afraid of what was going to happen to him every time we got in the car. I realized that as adults we want the same thing. We are afraid of the unknown and we want to know where we are going. We want to feel secure.

Most of us plan the course of our lives but there is no guarantee our life will run smoothly. Unexpected obstacles are thrown in front of us. Sometimes we experience struggles that we did not anticipate. We often become afraid of the unknown.

God assures us that He will always be with us, that He will direct our paths in the way that we should go. He will lead and guide us, teaching us as we go. All we have to do is trust Him and we will be "okay."

Prayer: "Thank you Father for guiding me and for providing the security I crave. Give me patience to understand the needs of others and do what I can to help them feel safe and secure. Amen."

Stepping Stones:

The Bible teaches us that God will always be with us. Do you desire the security in life that only God can provide? Do you realize that He will guide you in the way you should go? In what ways have you witnessed His hand at work in your life?

_____

_____

_____

_____

_____

_____

_____

_____

_____

_____

_____

_____

_____

TRIPPING OVER MY BOTTOM LIP

by Mary Edwards

The righteous cry out, and the Lord hears them; He delivers them from all their troubles. The Lord is close to the brokenhearted and saves those who are crushed in spirit. (Psalm 34:17-18 NIV)

****

At a church gathering, a member approached where I was sitting, paused, and then moved to another table and sat next to someone else. My mind quickly ran through a litany of unwanted questions. *Wonder what that was about? There is plenty of room at this table. What have I done to her?* It only took a few minutes of that kind of thinking to drain every ounce of my self-esteem. I could feel a mild depression coming on.

Rather than give in to those feelings I whispered a quick prayer and asked God to set my mind back in focus. I refused to permanently grab hold of the down feelings and I wasn't really being rejected, even though it felt like that. Satan wanted me to feel bad about myself and build anger toward my friend. I remembered some good advice from years before: other people's issues are not my own.

The Holy Spirit listened to my prayer and comforted the ache as He ministered to me, "Think with your head and not with your heart. Trust me with this." He placed a God-sized bandage on my little boo-boo of pride.

How often this happens to me when I put assumptions in front of facts and give satan an opening to creep in and stir up my emotions. Thankfully, I know who has control over fixing the cracks.

Prayer: "Heavenly Father, thank you for showing me that I am not always seeing the full picture. Lord, thank you for showing me that what I see and what I feel isn't always what is happening. Keep my eyes open and my pride in check. Thank you, God, for sending the Holy Spirit to ease the pains that everyday life can throw at me. Please help me when I trip over my bottom lip that I only fall straight into Your compassionate care. In Jesus' name, Amen."

Stepping Stones:

Have you ever assumed the worst of someone just to find out satan was doing his best to discourage you through them? When your feelings are hurt, and you are brokenhearted, how has God worked to reconcile the relationship?

_____

_____

_____

_____

_____

_____

_____

_____

_____

_____

_____

STILL STANDING

by Annette Gates

The righteous face many troubles but the Lord rescues them from each and every one. (Psalm 34:19 NLT)

****

There's a fairy tale making the rounds that has people living happily ever after when they give their lives into God's control. Unfortunately, we don't live in a fairy tale and the truth of the matter is the righteous face many difficulties in life. As observed by the Psalmist, however, the Lord rescues us from every challenge that comes our way.

Well into my third year of widowhood I can testify that the righteous (I am made righteous by Christ's righteousness) do indeed encounter many troubles: blown truck engine, meals eaten alone, crumbling chimney, an empty chair on holidays, rotten window frames, solitary nights, freezing pipes, and I could go on for quite a while, but you get the idea. If I had believed the fairy tales I was hearing, I would have given up on God for letting these things happen, but it is, after all, a fairly tale and God has faithfully rescued me from the troubles of 916 days without my husband,

And I am still standing!

Prayer: "Thank you, dear Father, for your tender care. You are the One who knows my needs and answers my prayers. You rescue me with your mighty hand. Amen."

Stepping Stones:

Can you testify that you are still standing after coming through a trying time? Someone has said, "If you're going to make it in this world, you have to stick." Are you sticking with God?

_____

_____

_____

_____

_____

_____

_____

_____

_____

_____

_____

_____

_____

THE DESIRE OF MY HEART

by Mary Jane Downs

*Delight yourself in the Lord, and he will give you
the desires of your heart. (Psalm 37:4 ESV)*

****

I received the Billy Graham Training Center program guide today. As I thumbed through the speaker section, I came across my favorite author, Lloyd John Ogilvie. Years ago on a whim, I had ordered one of his books called *The Other Jesus* for a penny from a new book club. It was love from that first book. I appreciated the way he explained the love and care of God. I began to feel accepted and treasured by God as I finished one book after another. John Ogilvie's influence was a substantial catalyst in my quest for intimacy with God.

Mr. Ogilvie's written words are not the only cherished memory I have of him. The more I read his books, the more I desired to meet him. I lived in a small town in Louisiana and had no extra money so the chances of meeting him were next to impossible, or so I thought. However, that did not keep me from believing the impossible could happen. It was a dream I kept tucked away for "someday".

Two years later, to my surprise and joy, God met my heart's desire. It came at a time when I needed desperately to know that God was with me and that He was hearing my prayers.

The excitement started building when my husband came home one night and said, "You'll never guess who is coming to First United Methodist Church in Ruston, La.

"Who?"

"Lloyd John Ogilvie" he answered.

I screamed and jumped around the room with joy while my husband gave me his knowing smile. Ruston was only thirty minutes away and the three-night conference was free. I couldn't have asked for a more perfect answer to my dreams.

On the night of the first meeting, I was standing in a hallway, when the door beside me opened and a tall, handsome man came in. I immediately knew who it was as a broad smile crossed my face. Mr. Ogilvie extended his hand toward me and said, "Hi, I'm Lloyd John Ogilvie."

As I stood there talking with him, I knew by his loving responses that he believed what he wrote. The memory of that divinely appointed meeting has been a lasting testament that God knows the desires of my heart.

Do you have desires hidden deep within your heart? God is listening to those secret cries whether it seems like it or not. Don't give up on your God-inspired desires. Live with expectancy knowing that, when the time is right, God will answer.

Prayer: "Lord, help me believe in my dreams even when they seem impossible. Help me remember all things are possible with you. Amen."

Stepping Stones:

What are the desires of your heart? Do you have dreams that seem impossible? Can you trust God with them and wait patiently as He brings them to life?

_____

_____

_____

_____

_____

_____

_____

_____

_____

_____

_____

_____

_____

RENEWED

by Stella Rome Carroll

"Create in me a clean heart, O God; and renew a right spirit within me."
(Psalms 51:10 KJV)

****

My grandmother's Depression Era bedroom suit sat abandoned in my garage for at least five years. Dust and cobwebs gathered and hung freely around the legs and back and who knew what else had crept underneath and made a home there. There were scratches and chips in the wood. Not only that, my teenage son had placed a leaky can of motor oil on the side table.

I loved my grandmother's bedroom when I was growing up. A pure white chenille bedspread had adorned the bed and the bed posts held a turned wood elegance. White ruffled sheer curtains hung gracefully from the windows. The dresser mirror was adorned with engraved petite milky white flowers on the edges of the three piece bevel. Crocheted doilies lay across the slightly opened drawers on each side. A narrow strip of glass formed a shelf that held dainty bottles of perfume. On special occasions Grandma would pin up her hair and apply make-up while seated in front of the mirror. The mirrored wardrobe had deep drawers down the center and a place to hang clothes on each side. The stain of the furniture had a two tone affect that was very warm and inviting.

But now, the heart of the furniture had been dulled by neglect and abuse. Its shine was no longer visible. The life had been leeched out of it. I called a refinisher who picked it up and hauled it away. I told him there was no rush and he took me at my word. Finally, after nine months, he called to say it was ready for delivery.

When I saw it my heart skipped a few beats. My grandmother's bedroom suit had been restored! The sheen was back. The distinctive rich tones of the wood took on a depth that I had forgotten was there. The cobwebs were gone and so was the motor oil stain. I carefully placed new sheets across the new mattress and topped them with a quilted bedspread embroidered with petite wine colored flowers. I could almost see my grandmother sitting there in front of the mirror surrounded by all that warmth and majesty. With skillful and caring hands, the refinisher had brought life back to my grandmother's furniture and I could once again feel the splendor of each piece.

Prayer: "Father, please cleanse my heart of any neglect and abuse I have hidden within me. With your skillful and caring hands, replace it with a renewed spirit that is visible to others. Amen."

Stepping Stones:

When have you felt like my Grandmother's furniture; neglected, abused, covered in dust and stained by life? God sent His Son to bring restoration to His children. How has God worked to restore your beauty and shine? What has He done to encourage you and bring peace to your life?

_____

_____

_____

_____

_____

_____

_____

_____

_____

_____

_____

_____

THIS SIDE OF PARADISE

by Pamela McCormick

"Cast your burden on the Lord, and he will sustain you;"
(Psalm 55:22A ESV)

****

God has promised us abundant life here and now, on this side of paradise but sometimes the everydayness of life on this side is hard. Hear one lady's story:

Fingernails chewed to the quick, and cuticles beginning to bleed. A search for band-aids to hide what has been chewed away. Ironically, she is not searching for why so much anxiety is inside her. It is a fear, better not spoken, better kept contained, like a message in a bottle, than being exposed and naked for another's eyes to see.

Talk is almost non-existent. Simple questions like, "What are you doing?" and "What do you want to watch on television?" characterize the relationship. Desiring the other's opinion or asking about another's well-being is too intimate and threatening to the safety of the union.

Happiness seems an impossible dream. Everyone else experiences it, but not her. She tells herself it's just not in the cards. Every morning she wakes up hoping that this will be the day when things are different, but then she remembers, she is on this side of Paradise.

The most wonderful words her ears could hear are "How are you?" That would indicate there was some concern about whether she existed or not. Giving this person what they need has been her one link to their love, and yet why is this link in the chain broken? Is it a call to escape, because things are broken, or is it a sign that mending is needed to start anew?

What should she do with something broken? Instinct would have her see it beyond repair and cause her to grab the dust pan and the broom and sweep all the broken pieces up and throw them away. But then she recognizes that not all the links are broken. A few are still intact. Is this a sign of hope for ongoing commitment, despite what one broken link in the chain offers? Is God calling her to freedom, or is His call one of peace, not broken pieces?

God then reminds her: Was it not brokenness that caused her to find Him on this side of Paradise? If He could take care of her then, He can take care of this, too? So she prays that she would trust Him, knowing He can do more with her little bit of faith than she can do with her slice of homegrown fear? She may be on this side of Paradise, but so are YOU, GOD. You're with her, until the end. She doesn't know what will be, but she knows the One who wills all things to be.

Prayer: "Gracious Lord of Life, thank you for seeing my cares as important and being willing to bear them for me. Thank you for living on this side of Paradise with me and restoring the broken-hearted, the down-trodden and the helpless. Amen."

Stepping Stones:

Is there brokenness in your life; broken relationships, broken dreams, broken finances, broken health, broken heart? Do you know that God cares about your brokenness? Can you testify to ways that God has healed your broken pieces? If healing still needs to happen, cry out to the Great Healer, mender of dreams and broken hearts.

_____

_____

_____

_____

_____

_____

_____

_____

_____

_____

_____

_____

A JUMPER CABLES KIND OF DAY

by Mary Jane Downs

Whom have I in heaven but you? And there is nothing on earth that I desire besides you. My flesh and my heart may fail, but God is the strength of my heart and my portion forever. (Psalm 73:25 NIV)

****

We've all been there. Running late, we jump in the car and speed to our destination. We arrive at an appointment, with seconds to spare. We're so proud of ourselves for accomplishing that feat. Then we return to the car to find that we left our lights on, the battery is dead and all we get when we turn the key is that sickening click-click-click sound. If we have jumper cables, they are in another vehicle so we look around the parking lot for someone to help us.

We all need infilling and refueling as we travel the "Road of Righteousness". I hope that as you read this song I wrote, you will feel a power surge from the Holy Spirit Himself. The song has no ascribed tune yet. However, as you read over and ponder the words, I pray the right tune for you will become evident.

> I woke up just a moanin'
>
> But I knew I had to keep a goin'.
>
> My spirit felt on empty
>
> So to my Bible, I went a searchin'.

Soon the power was a surgin'

Cause Your words began emergin'.

It only took a few peaceful moments

In Your Presence to feel energized again.

Chorus:

It was a jumper cables kind of day.

I needed a jolt from you, Lord, just to start me on my way.

Drained of all the power on the trials of yesterday

So I needed a recharging before I headed out today.

The red line revs up the bloodline

And the black one is the prayer line.

When both these are connected,

Double power is sent from heaven.

Keep a tight check on the grippers

So the infilling can be quicker.

Soon my spirit starts a revvin'

Cause my soul has received the blessin' (to go forth).

Begin your day with a scripture, a song or a melody in your heart. Even though your quiet time with the Lord each day may seem like it cost you, in the end, it will actually save you and keep you on the path towards victory.

Prayer: "Lord, strengthen me this day and everyday to do your will for my life. Teach me that in Your presence I have everything I need. Amen."

Stepping Stones:

What do you do when you are feeling run down, powerless? What can I do today and throughout this week that will help me charge up and maintain my spiritual batteries?

_____

_____

_____

_____

_____

_____

_____

_____

_____

_____

_____

_____

_____

IT STARTED WITH A SMILE

by Mary Edwards

Declare His glory among the nations, His marvelous deeds among all people. (Psalm 96:3 NIV).

****

"Hey, how ya doing Mary?" my friend asked.

"Hey, I'm doing real well. How are you?"

"What are you so smiley about? You always have that smile." she said, returning a smile of her own.

I pushed my grocery cart past the stand of apples and right there in front of the grapes I went up to her and said, "It's a God thing." Happy expressions grew bigger. With raised eye brows she invited more explanation. My face painted itself a blushing pink as the thrill of telling my story grew inside of me. "I am so excited about what God has done in my life lately. A lot of healing is going on."

Her wide eyes asked for more.

"In November, after being married for 30 years, I finally told my husband about the abuses I suffered as a child and now I am able to share about what God has done through all of this."

She placed her hand on her chest and with a deep sigh and a purposeful grin she said, "You never know," she paused, "you never really know who has been through abuse and who needs to hear of your faith."

"Oh, you are right, but sometimes you do know."

She gave me a wink and told me an abbreviated version of her own story. I felt her joy as she expressed her awe at the love of God and His rescue in her life.

We shared of overcoming the same issues and both of us boiled over in praises to God. We talked about educating people about child sexual abuse. But even more we shared victory stories of how gracious and caring our Heavenly Father is. "Woo Hoo! God is so GOOD!" You would have thought we were cheerleaders standing there among the grapes and tomatoes. Both of us desire to be the ministering disciples God instructs us to be. And we were doing just that.

"Oh how I loved having church here with you today," she said as we departed.

Yes, right there beside the onions, peppers, bananas and celery, we had church. The Holy Spirit conversed in our hearts, we worshipped the greatness of God and joy was present.

It started with a smile that started with Him.

Prayer: "Heavenly Father, no matter what door I enter, please enter it first. Let me be aware that I am opening the door for you. Help me display Your love and mercy. Please help me be gentle and bold as I present myself as a witness of Your greatness. In the precious name of Jesus, I pray. Amen."

Stepping Stones:

When has your smile encouraged a conversation with someone? Do people see Jesus when they look at you? Do you take Him with you wherever you go? Do you go anywhere that Jesus wouldn't be welcome? What could you do this week to make His reflection shine brighter in you?

_____

_____

_____

_____

_____

_____

_____

_____

_____

_____

_____

_____

THE LIGHTED PATH

by Carolyn Wease

Thy word is a lamp unto my feet, and a light unto my path.
(Psalm 119:105 KJV)

****

A precious missionary friend told me of an extraordinary event she experienced during her time in the mission field. Mamie began her missionary journey when just a young woman and happily devoted over 30 years of her life as a missionary to the Native American Indians in Arizona. She had endless stories of miraculous events that took place during the years she lived within the tribes of that region. One specific story left a vivid image imprinted on my mind.

On one particular evening, after a day spent working with some young people from one of the villages, she and another missionary were traveling back to their home when their car broke down. With no phone available and no houses nearby to find help, they contemplated staying put until someone came looking for them but then decided to start walking. Even though this was a remote area with little chance of anyone passing by, they knew sooner or later someone would come to look for them. As they walked, night fell but they continued walking, passing the time talking about the goodness of God.

At one point, as they were walking, they realized the road under their feet appeared to be well lit and they could see clearly where they were going. Even though it was totally dark around them, they were able to see the road clearly. Stunned by this fact they both stopped walking. As they did the road quickly became dark again and they could no longer see where to walk. Not really sure if it was their imagination playing tricks on them, they started walking again to see what would happen. As they did, once again, there was a light that shone on the road where they were walking. They tried stopping and starting several times and each time it was the same. As long as they continued to walk they were able to see, but when they stopped and began to look around, the darkness of the road overtook them. Realizing that God was lighting their way, they had a shouting time right there in the middle of the road. They were still rejoicing when they were located by their group, giving God praise for giving them a lighted path that night to show them the way.

Prayer: "Help us walk in the light of your Word, Lord, not wavering by circumstances around us. Your Word is our road map. No matter how dark our path may seem, we can still see where to walk if we let the light of your Word lead us. Amen."

Stepping Stones:

Spend extra time reading God's Word this week. As you do, ask Him to illuminate your mind and open your understanding. Receive the light He shines on your path. What scripture verses touched your heart this week?

_____

_____

_____

_____

_____

_____

_____

_____

_____

_____

_____

_____

LET ME TELL YOU A THING OR TWO

by Pamela McCormick

"Blessed are all who fear The Lord, who walk in His ways."
(Psalm 128:1 NIV)

****

Have you ever wanted to give someone a piece of your mind? Do hearing the words, "Let me tell you a thing or two," make you cringe? Normally these words are negatively associated with setting things straight between two opposing parties.

For me, a message of blessing, called perspective is heard. It requires that I desire to grow and hold my tongue in obedience to God's call above all else. My words can be used to help or hinder another person's walk. Saying too much is similar to stuffing acorns into a chipmunk's mouth. Giving someone a piece of my mind can damage a person's self-worth. That's why everything we say should be salted with grace. Isn't that how God responds to us?

I've heard these excuses and used them myself: "But you don't know how they acted; you don't know what they did; I have a right to stand up for myself, don't I?" I often convince myself that my way is the best way, but then I ask myself if I am going to live a life of seek and destroy or a life God says is pleasing in His sight? If I choose to burn someone else's candle to the ground, it doesn't make my candle burn any brighter.

Do I always try to get in the last word? I've learned that the final word is not mine and never will be. The final word is God's and I find it by resting in The One that can save me from my enemies and from myself. By insisting on having everything my way, I am not trusting God's ability to fix what seems to me to be an irreparable situation.

By living life my way, I am not taking hold of the power available to me to live life God's way. Until I recognize my need for God's help, I will continue to see others as broken pieces that I want removed from my life so my life will be better. God wants me to see what He's trying to teach me through the uniqueness of the other person. He may have placed that person in my life to act as sandpaper to smooth out my rough edges. As I surrender to Him, I'm saying, "Yes, God. Go ahead and tell me a thing or two. I'm listening."

Prayer: "Dear God, forgive me when I don't see Your higher purpose. Teach me Lord, to listen to You and walk with You. In You is life and peace and salvation. Fill me with Your Power so I can live, not as I think best, but according to Your will for me. Thank You God for teachable moments. Amen."

Stepping Stones:

What situation is going on in your life that you have not trusted God to take care of? Is there a difficult person you are dealing with? Do you trust God to handle the reconciliation and restoration that is needed?

_____

_____

_____

_____

_____

_____

_____

_____

_____

_____

_____

_____

_____

QUESTIONS FOR GOD

by Rachel Critchley

The fear of the Lord is the beginning of knowledge, but fools despise wisdom and instruction. (Proverbs 1:7 NIV)

****

As a youngster, I remember being told that there will be a time when we can speak to God and He will answer all of our questions. My inquisitive mind was full of questions that needed answers:

What happened to the Lost Colony?
What really occurred on the Grassy Knoll when John Kennedy was killed?
Where on Earth was the Garden of Eden?

I actually made a list of questions I wanted God to answer for me. My special list was kept on my dresser and was added to as questions came to my mind. It never occurred to me that I would not have this list with me after my death, but I did not worry about that small detail then.

As an adult I realize I need to have any specific questions memorized. The questions I will be concerned with then will not require memorization. I am looking forward to knowing the "whys" behind the things in life I do not now understand. As a Christian, I know there is a greater plan and I am not supposed to understand everything this side of Heaven. I'd like the fog to clear just a little though so I can understand more. As I read, study, and learn, some things become clearer. Eventually all will be crystal clear.

"For now we see only a reflection as in a mirror; then we shall see face to face. Now I know in part; then I shall know fully, even as I am fully known" (1 Corinthians 13:12 NIV). As I mature as a Christian, I realize that as I step into Heaven and see Jesus, the only thing on my mind will be bowing down before Him in worship. Then we'll have all of eternity together to learn from Him as He continues to nurture us in the faith.

Prayer: "Lord, please help me understand more as my journey as a Christian continues. I know eventually I will understand all. For now, help me be content to keep trying to learn more of your teachings and to be the best I can be for You. Amen."

Stepping Stones:

What questions would you like God to answer for you? Make your list here. Then praise God that you won't have any questions on your mind when you step into Heaven and see Jesus on that glorious day.

_____

_____

_____

_____

_____

_____

_____

_____

_____

_____

_____

GUARD YOUR HEART

by Carolyn Wease

Above all else, guard your heart, for everything you do flows from it.
(Proverbs 4:23 NIV)

****

At the close of a Sunday morning sermon, our Pastor asked each of us to place one hand over our hearts while we prayed and asked God to search our hearts. As I prayed earnestly, willing to hear anything God might say to me, He warmed me with his presence. As I stood in His loving embrace, I heard the words, "Guard your heart." His message held urgency, as in a flashing sign on the road warning of danger ahead. "Tell my people to guard their hearts."

In that moment, God showed me that many of his people have permitted worldly things to infiltrate their heart and can no longer see or appreciate the blessings he has given them. Our heart is where we hold our desires, our will, and the choices that make us who we are. God gives us instructions to help us guard our hearts from danger. He tells us to be careful what we speak (don't partake in corrupt conversation), where we look (keep our eyes straight ahead and on Him, not getting distracted by enticements of the flesh), and where we walk (go only places you know God would be pleased with).

The slide toward worldliness can be very subtle, almost unnoticeable. Choosing movies and television shows with violence and bad language, listening to off-color jokes at work to be part of the crowd, relying on horoscopes to guide our days, falling away from our daily Bible reading in favor of magazines and others books, or simply missing church on Sunday to pursue other seemingly innocent activities with our families, and the list goes on.

There is an enemy who is out to steal, kill and destroy us in whatever way he can. When we let down our guard and become centered on things of this world, the enemy is waiting to steal from us. The danger is that what we allow him to steal may one day be impossible to re-claim.

Prayer: "God, help us guard our heart with all our might and hold tight to what you have blessed us with. Help us keep our heart centered on you and resist the enticements of this world that could cause us to lose everything we hold dear. Amen."

Stepping Stones:

Have you compromised your Christian beliefs and bought into the pull of the world? Do the places you frequent, the way you treat people, and your speech prove to others that you are committed to Jesus? Have you allowed satan to steal from you? How can you reclaim it?

_____

_____

_____

_____

_____

_____

_____

_____

_____

_____

_____

ALL DOGS GO TO HEAVEN

by Mary Jane Downs

A righteous person cares even about the life of his animals.
(Proverbs 12:10 NIV)

****

Two years ago, I woke up, grabbed Maggie, my dachshund, and put her on the floor, then headed to the kitchen. After awhile, I noticed Maggie hadn't followed me into the kitchen as she normally did. Curious to see what she was up too, I went to investigate. There she was right where I had left her. She would not move. She attempted to stand but she obviously couldn't.

The veterinarian's office did tests and x-rays. When the doctor invited me into his office for the consultation, I knew the prognosis was not good. As He clipped the x-ray over the light he explained that Maggie's back was deteriorated to the point that she could not walk. He could give her some back treatments that would help her temporarily, but surgery was not advised. When he said she was in a lot of pain, I felt horrified. The doctor didn't mentioned putting her to sleep until I asked what he would do. He said it was my decision. I decided to do the back treatments simply because I was not ready to let Maggie go yet.

Over the next couple of days, I prayed and agonized over what to do. I did not like this 'live or die' decision-making. While I was out on the porch the next afternoon, the Lord gave me a vision. I saw His hands come down and take Maggie as he spoke: "Here, let me take care of her for awhile." Peace flooded my soul as I realized she was heaven bound.

The next morning when I took Maggie outside, she looked at me, her eyes barely open, and I sensed her say: "I will be here for you as long as I can but I am tired and ready to go home." Maggie was at the vet's office within the hour.

Now, it was happening again with Buddy. His knees were badly deteriorated. We tried the pain meds the Vet recommended for two weeks but they were making him sick. I knew what needed to be done. Again, I saw the Lord's hands come down. My daughter and I took Buddy out to the local Christian camp for one last romp. He swam in the lake and frolicked like a pup. It did my heart good to see how Buddy enjoyed life right up to the end.

Our pets bring us joy, alter our perspective, and give us loyalty and devotion like no other. When we lose them, it feels like we have lost our best friend. If it has happened to you, take time to grieve and then take time to remember where it all began.

Prayer: "Lord, help those who have lost someone close to them, either person or pet. Comfort them with your blanket of love and bring them gently through their grief. Amen."

Stepping Stones:

Have you lost someone close to you? How has God helped you overcome the loss? Record memories that make you smile here.

_____

_____

_____

_____

_____

_____

_____

_____

_____

_____

_____

_____

_____

FROM DEATH TO HOPE

by Mary Edwards

In the way of righteousness is life, and in its pathway there is no death.
(Proverbs 12:28)

****

D.J. at fifteen months old, was the picture perfect little boy, with my eyes and his daddy's smile; his sister's best friend. His colicky tummy caused us all to cry. Did he cry because I did?

Postpartum depression enslaved me. Thoughts of divorce swirled in my head. If that happened, would my children be taken from me? I feared a continued 'hell on earth life' if I left. Excuses helped me justify my sad, sick mind. It made sense to me. End it and hurt no more. No one would ever hurt my boy if I took him with me in death.

D.J. looked so darling in his cutest outfit. I wanted him to look like the angel he is when they found us. My plan seemed easy: Put my baby in his car seat, turn the ignition switch on and cry myself to sleep as I allowed asphyxiation to choke us into the grave. Sadness gone forever.

Looking into D.J.'s beautiful brown eyes, we moved toward the garage. He looked at me and grinned but I could no longer focus on him through the tears in my eyes. I was determined to follow through with my plan. My hand froze on the garage door. I couldn't turn back, nor go forward. I fell to the ground as the Holy

Spirit moved within me. His love overcame every feeling of depression. I could feel God hold me as I held on to my little boy.

"I am so sorry, God. Help me," I whispered. God held me in his arms as we got up and walked back inside the house. Tears dampened D.J.'s head as we sat in the recliner. Holding my sweet, innocent child against my chest, we rocked and rocked and fell asleep in the peacefulness of the presence of the Lord.

I knew then that I could rely on God to pull me through this darkness. The Holy Spirit is constant. He is available to help us out of what feels like the bottomless pits of life. He is available every minute, every hour, and every day.

My son is now twelve. When I look in his eyes I see life. I see a blessing from God. I see joy. It's a gift to feel love. God is gracious while He waits for all of us to know and accept His love.

Prayer: "Father, I ask for continued peace and heart healing. Help those who feel suicidal. Protect them, Lord, and ease their pain. Give them hope in You, hope in healing and a trust in Your love. In Jesus' name. Amen."

Stepping Stones:

Have you ever experienced depression or desperation that caused you to make decisions you regretted? When you are in the dark, where do you find the light that leads you to safety? How can you help others in desperate situations?

REDIRECTED

by Annette Gates

We can make our plans, but the Lord determines our steps.
(Proverbs 16:9 NLT)

****

Shopping list made. Coupons ready. Library books gathered. Returns and receipts matched up. Dry cleaning gathered and bagged up. Teeth brushed and flossed extra clean for my dentist's appointment. My route efficiently planned out so as not to waste time or gas. My plan for the day is ready to execute. Let's go. A few miles down the road traffic is stopped dead still. What is the holdup? Why is traffic at a standstill? You're kidding me! When did they decide to repair this bridge? Why wasn't the public informed so they could choose an alternate route? Grrrr.

How many times has your well-planned day been redirected by something you hadn't planned for? In our humanity, our first reaction is at least a little road rage. We have a tendency not to see God at work in every little detail of our lives. After all, isn't He too big and too busy for that? The truth is He's so in love with us that He wants to be involved in all the minute details of our lives.

During the years I operated "Mom's Taxi Service" for my daughters, I personally experienced having my path in traffic redirected only to find out later there had been a horrific accident on my normal route. God had determined the steps needed to preserve my life.

I've learned to keep my life fluid and look to see what God is doing when He changes my plans to His plans. I've been truly blessed as I notice how He weaves Himself into my life, even the tiniest parts.

Prayer: "Precious, loving Father, help me to see you in everything, big and small. Build my faith and increase my peace as I yield to Your direction. Thank you, ABBA. I love you. Amen."

Stepping Stones:

Has God ever redirected your plans? How did you handle the change? Do you realize that even though you are a tiny dot in the universe, He knows where you are? He knows your name, how many hairs are on your head, and He cares for you? How does that make you feel?

_____

_____

_____

_____

_____

_____

_____

_____

_____

_____

_____

_____

MAKING RIGHT CHOICES

by Carolyn Wease

*A man's heart plans his way, but the Lord directs his steps.
(Proverbs 16:9 NKJV)*

****

Choices are a part of our everyday lives. Some choices are simple and require little effort, like what to have for breakfast or what outfit to wear. Others take more deliberation, such as what car to buy or how to plan a social event. Then there are those that I consider major choices that might affect the course of our lives, like where to attend college, career moves, whom to date, whom to marry, or when to start a family. Often we are reluctant to choose when facing life affecting decisions. We're afraid we will choose the wrong one and later regret our decision.

Many times when facing major life decisions, I've struggled to determine what was best. I prayed and asked God for direction, made a list of all my pros and cons, and asked every reliable person I knew for advice. Still a cloud of desperation would hang over me as the deadline drew sickeningly near and I remained unsure what to do. Even after making the best choice I could, I have been known to cry out, "God, I've done the best I can with this decision. If I am making the wrong choice here, please close the door of opportunity so I can't go through and open up another." Thankfully, somehow God has always helped me through each and every decision and remarkably pointed me in the right direction.

I finally concluded one day that God wants his children to be happy as we live our life in fellowship with Him. If we seek to please him in all we do, He will guide us by his word and his Holy Spirit to make right choices, even if it means closing some doors to us. As we plan our lives and make our choices we should do so under his direction, knowing that He has a master plan and it is a good one.

Prayer: "God, I know that you have a plan for my life, a good plan to prosper me, give me hope and a future (Jeremiah 29:11 TLB). Thank you for the comfort in knowing that even with all the planning and choices I have to make in life, you will still intervene and direct my steps. Amen."

Stepping Stones:

Make a list of things you are facing right now that require making a decision. Pray over them, asking for God's guidance. Spend time with Him this week and expect answers. Record them here.

_____

_____

_____

_____

_____

_____

_____

_____

_____

_____

_____

_____

_____

_____

TREASURE HUNTING

by Mary Edwards

A man who has friends must himself be friendly, but there is a friend who sticks closer than a brother. (Proverbs 18:24 NKJV)

****

"The only way to have a friend is to be one."

Ralph Waldo Emerson

We have so much in common. Hanging out at the thrift store Saturday morning, I met Diane, the mother of an 11 year old boy, just like me. She finds treasures in someone else's trash, just like I do. I liked her telling me that she can walk out of there and feel like a million dollars. She praised God over a fixed toe. I found that a little "different" to tell a total stranger, but I accepted her conversation. It was just an open door: one God opened. I instantly liked Diane. I had only talked to her for about ten minutes but by the time we were through we were new sisters.

I am still in awe of how God works. Diane shared with me about needing prayer for her son. He went through a situation that she said was hard to explain. I reached out for a gentle hand shake and said, "Let me introduce myself, I am Mary Edwards, the founder of Be a Voice for Kids to help educate, prevent and heal child sexual abuse through the love of the Lord." Diane cried as I put my arm around her shoulder and hugged her and whispered a prayer of encouragement and healing over this hurting mother.

She told me our meeting was appointed by God himself. She gave me few details but enough to know we were meant to meet at that exact day, exact hour and exact huggable time. We exchanged phone numbers, said our farewells and "It was so nice to meet you's" and left each other with warm smiles.

We have chatted a couple of times since that God inspired first meeting and we're each lifting the other up, holding the other one close to our hearts. We both feel God's blessing in our meeting. I pray that God helps me find more thrifty sisters like Diane to encourage. The rewards in treasure hunting for Him are endless.

Prayer: "Dear Lord, Thank you for providing the right words to say. It is only through You and Your strength that I am able to share of healing. Lord, whenever you want me to speak to someone, let me have open ears to hear You. Thank you, Heavenly Father, for guiding our paths so that we all can grow closer in our relationship with You. In Jesus Name, Amen."

Stepping Stones:

How does God let you know when it's time to speak for Him? Have you had divine appointments that you know only God could have orchestrated? Record some of the highlights here and thank God for being real in your life and having a real plan suited just for you.

_____

_____

_____

_____

_____

_____

_____

_____

_____

_____

_____

_____

DINNER AND A WORKOUT

by Rachel Critchley

It is dangerous to have zeal without knowledge,
and the one who acts hastily makes poor choices. (Proverbs 19:2 NET)

****

Gatlinburg, Tennessee is a beautiful area in the Great Smoky Mountains National Park. My husband and I love to go there on vacation. It is a great place to relax and refresh.

On one trip I went a few days early and my husband was to follow when he could. The restaurant I picked that first evening was known to have some fun, out-of-the-ordinary eating areas. I was following the hostess to a seat when I saw a table whose chair was an actual swing. It looked so inviting I asked if I could sit there and the hostess quickly agreed.

As I took my "seat" the unique dining experience slowly unfolded. The seat was comfortable and relaxing as it gently swayed back and forth but, unless my feet were planted firmly on the floor, I was moving. And then the food arrived. What looked to be such an adorable place to eat turned out to be work. Moving to and fro and balancing my food on a fork, or even a spoon, didn't work so well. The entire meal involved using my leg and foot muscles to keep the swing from moving so my food was at an appropriate distance from my face. I got dinner and a workout for the price of one!

I could have asked to move but, since I requested the table, I felt an obligation to stay. Swings are fun but they have their place. It certainly is not at a table during a meal and particularly not in public. In life we often see something exciting and cute and initially believe it to be a good choice but the consequences are different than expected. What something seems to be and the reality of what it really is can be distinctly different. This meal reinforced the fact for me that in life I need to consider my choices thoroughly.

Prayer: "God, give me the wisdom to make wise choices in my life. Please help me consider the consequences of each decision I make so that I bring glory to You. I pray my actions speak loudly about my beliefs. Amen."

Stepping Stones:

Have you made choices that didn't work out the way you expected? How do you handle negative consequences so they won't happen again?

_____

_____

_____

_____

_____

_____

_____

_____

_____

_____

_____

_____

_____

SEND ME

by Stella Rome Carroll

Then I heard the voice of the Lord saying, "Whom shall I send? And who will go for us?" and I said, "Here am I. Send me!" (Isaiah 6:8 NIV)

****

As a young member of Trinity Baptist Church, I had finally grasped the passion of others for serving God. For months, as I had listened in Sunday school and in the worship service, my vulnerable heart had been touched and I had gone forward one Sunday morning committing my life wholly and completely to my heavenly Father.

I didn't know how to go about serving God or how I could "fit in" to working in our church but I felt a strong pull that I should be giving of myself. I didn't know what skills I had that would be useful and I certainly didn't know how to go about finding a way to be a help to anyone. I just kept feeling an urge to take a leap into God's plan.

It wasn't long before I noticed that there were a few individuals going around asking members to fill positions for the upcoming church year. They would pass right by me. No one even seemed to notice me. I kept wondering, "Is there not a job I can do?"

A few days later, at a church dinner, I overheard two ladies talking. "We haven't found anyone to work with the GA's yet," one of them said. The other one added, "I don't know of anyone that wants to work with those girls." I had two young sons of my own but I had a desire to work with young girls.

I had been praying, asking God to give me some direction if He was indeed calling me to give of myself to His church. I had not heard Him answer me, but after listening to these two ladies discussing their inability to find a GA leader, I asked God to give me the courage to speak up. I took a deep breath and stepped forward and boldly asked, "Can I work with the GA's." The surprise on their faces was evident. "Do you mean you want to be a GA leader?" asked the ladies.

They assured me that I could have the job. I worked with those Girls in Action, ages six through twelve, several years and I loved every challenging minute of it. Later I taught Sunday school, grades four through six and now I teach Adults. I know God called me into His ministry and the joy I have received has been tremendous. I am reminded many times of that bold step I took when I read Isaiah 6:8 "Here am I. Send me!"

Prayer: "Dear Father, I am truly grateful that you called me into your ministry and that you give me the courage to leap into your plan. Amen."

Stepping Stones:

The first move in following God's will is simply finding the courage to make the first move. List the ministries you have a passion for. List the talents and experiences God has given you that might help in your ministry work?

WONDERFUL COUNSELOR

by Annette Gates

For a child is born to us, a son is given to us. And the government will rest on His shoulders. These will be His royal titles: Wonderful Counselor, Mighty God, Everlasting Father, Prince of Peace.
(Isaiah 9:6 NLT)

****

What encouraging news! I have a wonderful counselor. This passage of scripture is quite familiar to many. You may have sung along as you heard this line in Handel's Messiah. I have a tendency to become so familiar with words that I stop thinking about what is being said.

Today a radio ministry challenged it's listeners to consider whether we qualify to call Messiah our Wonderful Counselor. His contention is that unless our actions support our words, we don't really believe what we are saying. My actions don't make Him any less a Wonderful Counselor, for He is still fully available. They do determine whether He is truly my Wonderful Counselor. I was challenged to make the choice to fully receive His counsel and to act on it.

I can certainly recall creating consequences that were not what I hoped for by following my own counsel, or even the advice of other well meaning individuals. Let's see, there was that awful prom night when I went with a boy out of pity. I felt so noble. I was miserable later on when he continued to pursue a relationship with me. That wasn't supposed to be part of the deal.

Then there was the time I was joy riding and nearly got stuck in a muddy road. The terror I felt at the prospect of having to explain to my Daddy why the car was mired in the mud was anything but joyful. You are probably recalling some instances of your own so I won't go on and on with mine.

Just imagine the difference it would make in our lives if all decisions and actions were determined by His perfect choices. The great news is, even if we've drifted away, we're always welcome to come to Him for counsel. It's His joy to receive us. He truly is a Wonderful Counselor.

Prayer: "Wonderful Counselor, thank you for your eagerness to hear my requests for your help and your faithfulness to supply counsel. Help me to have the wisdom to seek you and apply your counsel. I look forward to walking in your counsel and having a grateful heart to thank you for the goodness it brings to my life. Amen."

Stepping Stones:

Do you avail yourself of God's wonderful counsel? What questionable decisions in your past came to your mind as you read this devotion? What were the consequences? Thank God today for being your Wonderful Counselor.

THE GREATEST STORY EVER TOLD

by Stella Rome Carroll

For unto us a child is born, unto us a son is given.
(Isaiah 9:6 KJV)

****

The second night I was a resident at Cleveland Pines Nursing Center, their annual Christmas play was performed by the residents. The play began with the Inn Keeper turning away Mary and Joseph. Then residents were rolled in with angel wings and halos of stars. They were followed by shepherds in their garb, using their canes instead of staffs. Then the wise men were rolled in with their gifts, to tell "The Greatest Story Ever Told."

There was no room in the Inn for baby Jesus, yet I came to the realization that Jesus had room for these residents in their wheel chairs with their afflictions. Whether they could speak or sing or not, God used each of them to put on this moving, spectacular play. Even the older male resident that talked about the wise men with their gifts of gold, "Frankenstein" and Myrrh stirred my emotions. I broke down with sobs knowing that God and His love were in this place. I would not have traded this one moment in time for being anywhere else in the world because it reminded me of just how much God loves each of us no matter what our condition, no matter what our affliction, and no matter where we live.

Prayer: "Dear Father, Thank you for the love that you have for each of us. Amen"

Stepping Stones:

If God can use these nursing home residents to share His message, what do you think He might be able to do through you? In what ways has He used you to share His great story with others?

_____

_____

_____

_____

_____

_____

_____

_____

_____

_____

_____

_____

STRESS REDUCTION

by Rachel Critchley

"The grass withers and the flowers fall, but the word of our God endures forever." (Isaiah 40:8 NIV)

****

I love to read. Reading excites me. It reduces any stress I might be feeling, helps me think logically, and is educational. Numerous years ago I was getting stressed at work and it occurred to me I had not read a book in a long time. I decided I should get back to reading daily, even if I could only manage ten pages with my busy schedule. Two bookmarks, one holding my place, and the second moved to where I should be if I did not have the time to read the ten pages that day, marked my progress. This helped me relax in the evenings.

I developed a habit of keeping a list of the completed books by title, the author's name and the date the book was finished. This would enable me to know which authors to read again and which authors to avoid. After several years, I was looking at my list to check how many books I had been reading. I counted over thirty-six books for each of the three previous years. Although I love reading, over thirty-six books a year seemed like a lot of books. This gave me a good and a bad feeling. I was impressed at the amount of books I had read yet I had never read the Bible all the way through. I thought if I could read thirty-six books each of the past three years, I should be able to read the Bible from cover to cover in the next year.

After much prayer, I decided to begin my Bible reading journey the next January. Several choices were involved. First, I had to determine which Bible version to read since I would be spending a great deal of time with that Bible. Second, I obtained a reading schedule to try to maintain. I did not want to get too far ahead or too far behind. Third, I found a friend to read with me the next year. Having a friend and accountability partner added validity to the experience.

January, the first, I began reading the first page of my Bible. I finished the last page on December the thirty-first. I enjoyed the deeper understanding of the Bible this gave me. Having a friend to discuss the passages with me as we went added insight and comprehension to the journey. I was able to accomplish something in my thirties that I thought would have to wait well past retirement because of the time requirement.

Prayer: "Thank you God for making this possible. Thank you for helping me gain the knowledge that, with your help, I have the time to accomplish goals. Help me include religious goals in my attempts to learn more about You. Amen."

Stepping Stones:

Have you read through the Bible? If so, what did you learn from the experience? If not, what obstacles are hindering you? Remember that you don't have to start in January and you don't have to finish in a year. There are two-year reading plans available.

_____

_____

_____

_____

_____

_____

_____

_____

_____

_____

_____

_____

RACING THROUGH THE STORM

by Mary Edwards

Do you not know? Have you not heard? The Lord is the everlasting God, the Creator of the ends of the earth. He will not grow tired or weary, and his understanding no one can fathom. He gives strength to the weary and increases the power of the weak. Even youths grow tired and weary, and young men stumble and fall; but those who hope in the Lord will renew their strength. They will soar on wings like eagles will run and not grow weary, they will walk and not be faint. (Isaiah 40:28-31 NIV)

****

It took a long time for me to come forth and say, "He did this to me. He did it for three years. I felt him break my body and my spirit repeatedly." What was it that made me yell until someone finally heard? At 14, I walked in on another helpless soul being ripped apart. Thunder rolled inside of me and the fight for rescue hit me like lightening. I stormed with hate that this was happening. It was time to put a stop to it all, at least for the two of us. I recently heard that one little boy, who I love very much, is being victimized. Flash backs occurred. Anger and hurt surfaced once more. And again, the storms of life rolled through my bones.

God sent a friend who had experienced childhood sexual abuse. We talked about the Lord and how God had never walked away. We gave each other hope with words of encouragement.

134

We lifted each other in prayer. God placed us in each other's path so that we would trip into each other's hearts. We shared God.

With all the studying, praying and digging deep into God's word, I became like a race horse, galloping through the rain to the finish line. I trotted past the sounds of thunder and the pain of the darts of memory that struck like lightening. It was a very long time before I felt ready to cross the finish line and turn my name from Victim to Victor. I still have to use much effort to move forward to the end. But with Jesus as my trainer, I will make it through the storm.

The prayer partner God sent me and I aren't keeping the same pace but we both have the same fight to endure and the same goal: to heal. Healing is a process and we all progress at different rates. I do need to be careful to not leave others behind in the rain.

Prayer: "Dear Lord, I am so thankful that you are here whenever we reach for you. Please help us run to you through the storms life brings our way. In Jesus Name, Amen."

Stepping Stones:

What storms are raining in your life? Has God sent you a special friend with a similar history? How has God helped you weather your storms?

_____

_____

_____

_____

_____

_____

_____

_____

_____

_____

_____

_____

_____

_____

STUCK IN A RUT

by Carolyn Wease

Forget the former things; do not dwell on the past.
See, I am doing a new thing. (Isaiah 43:18 -19 NIV)

****

My church recently observed our 32nd anniversary by having a Homecoming Day celebration. We spent the day remembering and honoring both past and present members for their loyal service to God and the church. Though some are no longer with us, their labors of love still inspire us.

We sang the older hymns that remind us of times when God has helped us and touched our lives in special ways. Some of the memories were life altering ones like when we realized we needed a Savior and the change that happened within us when we asked Jesus into our hearts. A different memory was triggered with each song we sang, and with every person honored. Some memories were of happy times, others of sad times. We remembered when we had been scared or intimidated, confused or mistaken. But with every memory there was always the constant reality that God was right there with us through it all, encouraging, guiding, interceding and blessing.

There is great encouragement in remembering the times when God blessed us or brought us through a hard time. It's good to remember and be grateful, but thankfully we don't have to rely on memories only. We don't have to get stuck in the past, relying

137

only on our memories. God is still working on behalf of his children today.

Today when we wake up, we can rejoice because God has given us a new day to serve Him and live in His Kingdom. His mercies and compassions are new every day. We can live an abundant life, both here and in eternity. We can expect to see God's mighty hand working in our lives today.

We can joyfully look toward the future in anticipation of the mighty acts of God we are yet to see. Because we experienced His faithfulness in the past, we can count on it in the days ahead. He is the same yesterday, today and tomorrow. His love and care for us never ends.

Prayer: "Lord, though we rejoice in memories of past blessings and miracles, help us to expect to see new blessings and miracles even greater in our lives today than what we remember from the past. Amen."

Stepping Stones:

How has God brought you encouragement, guidance, blessings, and answered your prayers? Look back at the end of the week, and list the ways He's working in your life now.

_____

_____

_____

_____

_____

_____

_____

_____

_____

_____

_____

_____

_____

ONE STEP AT A TIME

by Stella Rome Carroll

You will go out in joy and be led forth in peace. (Isaiah 55:12 NIV)

****

Every morning I read my Bible and spend time praying to my Heavenly Father expressing my gratitude for His beautiful creation and for the many blessings that He has provided. I also request safety for my mother, my two sons, my two sisters and their families and those on our church prayer list.

I am in physical therapy twice per week and on those days I also ask God to give me the strength in my legs and feet to do the exercises. I admit to Him that I am afraid that I can't do them, afraid that my legs are too weak. My left leg becomes fatigued rather quickly and it drags and feels as if it's glued to the floor. The understanding therapist will kneel down and force my leg to take the next step. Even with holding onto the parallel bars and the therapist's assistance I have difficulty getting back to my wheel chair. I am so relieved when the session is over.

Everywhere I go people whiz by me. They take for granted the ability to walk. They put one foot forward and then the other without hesitation, without constantly watching their balance.

The therapist has been timing how long I can stand with and without assistance. My usual time is ten seconds without holding onto the parallel bars and thirty seconds holding on.

This morning as my nephew rolled me into the lobby, I noticed a plaque above the entrance to the therapy room, "Enter this place and go out in joy and be led forth in peace."(Isaiah 55:12) God spoke to me at that moment and I knew in my heart that he would give me the strength I needed to put each foot forward.

Again the therapist timed me. I stood without help fifteen seconds and I stood holding onto the parallel bars forty-five seconds! That small but important success encouraged me to keep going, to keep trying, to keep teaching Sunday school, to keep working on mission projects and to keep allowing God to use me despite my limitations. That morning, I left therapy with joy that encouraged me to let God lead me in peace.

Each of us endure obstacles or struggles at some point in our lives but with God leading us one step at a time we can be encouraged that even with our limitations His purpose will be accomplished.

Prayer: "Father, give us the strength and courage to tackle those barriers that seem to stand in our way. Help us graciously accept the gifts that you have given us, even when they don't seem like gifts. Let your purpose and peace surround us. Amen."

Stepping Stones:

God provides us with the strength and courage we need to face struggles. What struggles have you had that showed you God's hand at work on your behalf? Do you feel limited in any way? Where do you turn for help?

_____

_____

_____

_____

_____

_____

_____

_____

_____

_____

_____

_____

MIRACLE IN THE ICU

by Stella Rome Carroll

Heal me, O Lord, and I shall be healed. Jeremiah 17:14 (KJV)

****

The Assisted Living Center where my parents lived called me one Saturday afternoon in late July saying, "Your mom has passed out and has been sent by ambulance to the hospital." I wasted little time in heading to the hospital. When I arrived, the emergency room doctor explained that they were admitting Mama and had tests scheduled for Monday. My two sisters arrived and we kept a vigil in the waiting area over the weekend. On Monday, we were told she had a bleeding ulcer and needed surgery. Thankfully, the surgery was a success, but not too long afterward, Mama developed pneumonia. She was placed on a ventilator to help her breathe. This device is used for medical emergencies that require oxygen therapy.

She looked so frail and pale. She struggled for each breath as her bony chest heaved up and down. She was getting weaker and weaker and I told my sisters I didn't think she was going to make it. A nurse recommended that we think about removing Mama from the machine. Mama could not speak but she managed enough strength to motion with her hand that she was ready for us to remove it.

My sisters had cried all weekend but I held up well until the moment the doctor removed the device. Thoughts of *We're deciding her death. We're not God* filled my mind. I felt like screaming. I left ICU and ran down the hall to find a secluded spot. I sat down on a bench, and with tears flowing; I began to pray. Over and over I prayed, "Dear God, I know you still work miracles." A lady sat down beside me and listened to me talk about my mom, encouraging me with her words. I don't know who she was but I know she was an angel when I needed one.

Soon after she left my side, I returned to mom's bedside. My heart skipped a few beats when, to my astonishment, I realized Mama was improving! In a couple of days she was transferred to a nursing facility. A few months later the feeding tube was removed!

For a long time before the surgery, Mama had been someone who constantly whined and complained. You couldn't please her. It had gotten to the point I dreaded visiting her, but after her hospital stay her personality changed. She rarely complains now and I enjoy her company immensely. She lights up when I come to visit. I look forward to playing Scrabble with her every week, even though she wins nine out of ten games. I know God still provides miracles and I believe He granted a miracle that day so I could get to know and enjoy my mom once again.

Prayer: "Dear Father, I am grateful for your miracles! Thank you for the miracle of healing. Amen."

Stepping Stones:

God still provides miracles and grants them according to His purpose. What miracles have you evidenced in your life? Don't forget to list your salvation, a miracle only God can accomplish. Spend time thanking God this week for the miracles you've seen in your life and in the people around you.

_____

_____

_____

_____

_____

_____

_____

_____

_____

_____

_____

_____

DEM DRY BONES

by Pamela McCormick

"Then He said to me, "Prophecy to these bones and say to them, 'Dry bones, hear The Word of The Lord. I will make breath enter you, and you will come to life. Then you will know that I am The Lord."
(Ezekiel 37:4-5 NIV)

****

In a slump and discouraged, I listened to my doubts more than I was listening to God. I just couldn't make myself write, and then God did what only He could do. God breathed new life into these dry bones causing me to remember the gift He had given me. I am a writer and it is my choice to believe Him or to reject this gift

Who knew this dry period would lead to such a transformation in my heart and my spirit? My head kept telling me, "God, has forgotten all about you," and "You're not really a writer," and worst of all, "You will never get published." I put limits on God, basically telling Him, "You can't do this." It's okay, because I'm not the perfect one. He is, and He was going to do in me and through me what I couldn't do, because I chose to listen to Him and not to my negative thoughts.

This dry time, inundated with I cant's, I won't ever's, and ho hum, "it was just a dream anyway", was good. It helped me remember that God is still faithful in spite of all my doubts and fears. He is interested in helping me see the truth of how I should live, letting Him be God and yielding all the details to Him. Did my moaning, groaning, and complaining keep God from putting fresh breath in me? No. Finally, seeking God and His way, I surrendered all my doubts, fears, and inadequacies to Him. My focus turns to Jesus, and off of me. That's when miracles occurred.

I thought I would never start writing again. This dryness had gone on for many, many months when God whispered, "Turn your life and writing over to me, Pam, and I will make a way for you. It was tough but when God moved, these dry bones believed and now my dry bones are dancing. Put your hope in God. He will never fail you.

Prayer: "Thank You God that You are bigger than our doubts, bigger than our fears, and truly interested in our lives and what we do. Thank You God for answering prayers, spoken and unspoken. You are amazing, God. Amen."

Stepping Stones:

What are your dreams and hopes? Are there doubts, fears, disappointment or discouragement associated with them? What keeps you from turning everything over to God? Do you believe He can breathe life into your dry bones?

GOD WAS THERE FOR ME

by Lorna Hawley

The city will measure about 31,500 feet all the way around. From then on the city's name will be: Yahweh Shammah, meaning The Lord is There. (Ezekiel 48:35 NOG)

****

Cancer caused me to require major back surgery on December 31, 2008. My husband died very suddenly five weeks later. In 2012, another spot showed up. My oncologist was very concerned, but my surgeon said he believed it was nothing. *I can't go through another bout of cancer without my husband.* That way of thinking nearly consumed me, but then a change came over me as I began thinking about all that God had done for me and all the different ways He had taken care of me. I knew He would see me through whatever was ahead. My surgeon was right and the spot was nothing. I am cancer free; praise God! During those many months of uncertainty, I focused on God and experienced the deeper meaning of His names:

Jehovah: "I AM" He needs nothing and no one but He chooses to have a relationship with us and to love us forever as His children.

Jehovah-Jireh: The Lord will provide. Abraham first used this name when God provided a ram for a sacrifice in place of his son, Isaac. If God can provide a ram, part the Red Sea, keep sandals and clothes from wearing out for 40 years, make the walls of

Jericho fall with a shout, raise people from the dead; what is there that He cannot provide for us?

Jehovah-Nissi: The Lord is my Banner. God covers us and protects us from the world and satan. Psalm 91:4, "He shall cover you with His feathers, and under His wings you shall take refuge; His truth shall be your shield and buckler. He is the only protection we need."

Jehovah-Rapha: The Lord Who Heals. Jesus is the Great Physician who provides healing spiritually, physically, emotionally and mentally.

Jehovah-Rohi: The Lord is my Shepherd. We are like dumb sheep, but God lovingly leads us, provides for our needs, carefully guards and protects us.

Jehovah-Shalom: The Lord of Peace. Jesus is called the Prince of Peace in Isaiah 9:6. He will give us inner peace and harmony when we ask Him.

Jehovah-Shammah: The Lord is There. As God's children, He is always with us. He is not only in our now, but He is already in our future and has already figured that out for us.

We are His children. He will provide for all our needs, protect us, heal us, shepherd and guide us, fight our battles, fill us with His peace, is our constant companion Who will never desert us, and has provided us with His righteousness and an eternal home.

Prayer: "O God, You are a mighty God. As you reign from Heaven with wisdom, power and love, you care deeply for your children. Thank you for the many ways you shield and protect us and meet our needs. Amen."

Stepping Stones:

Which of these names of God particularly speaks to your heart today? Spend time this week thinking about the times God has been there for you. You are His child. He cares deeply for you. What do you need from His this week?

_____

_____

_____

_____

_____

_____

_____

_____

_____

_____

_____

_____

THE SOUND OF SINGING

by Cathy Biggerstaff

The Lord your God is with you, the Mighty Warrior who saves. He will take great delight in you; in his love he will no longer rebuke you, but will rejoice over you with singing." (Zephaniah 3:17 NIV)

✶✶✶✶

The worship was extravagant. Witnesses popped up here and there like kernels of popcorn in hot oil, encouraging the hearers, bringing assurance that God is working in our community. The Word was spoken, seeping into our hearts and reaching the hidden places. The Holy Spirit electrified the air in the sanctuary, bringing forth expectancy in and around the worshippers. Many found their way to the altar.

I was one of those kneeling there, sobbing, repenting of the sin of misusing my time. Even though I was doing good things, I wasn't spending my time doing what God wanted me to. I needed to learn to say "NO" to anything, even good things, that weren't where God wanted me to spend my energy. He impressed on my heart that just because I had the skills to do a job well didn't mean I was the one who was supposed to do it. My willingness to jump in and do a job was robbing others of the joy of doing them: another reason to repent.

And then I heard it, the sweet angelic music floating over my head. It took my breath away. I had to open my eyes to make sure I wasn't in Heaven instead of kneeling at the front pew. The voice

I heard came from a lady standing two rows back, oblivious to how it was affecting me.

God brought Zephaniah 3:17 to mind as a balm to soothe my burdened heart. That verse reminded me that He saved me and He takes great delight in me, warts and all. Because of His great love for me, He forgives and forgets my sins. Instead of the punishment I deserve, He rejoices over me with singing.

He doesn't show favorites among His children so He'll do the same thing for you. Meet Him at the altar and repent of your sins, then listen for the music.

Prayer: "Thank you, Lord, for the way you work to remind your children of your great love for us. Thank you for forgiveness and for mercy. Thank you for the way you rejoice over your less than perfect children with singing. Amen."

Stepping Stones:

What sins are you holding close and not repenting of? Is there a sin that brings you pleasure that you don't want to give up? Go ahead and give them to Jesus. He knows what they are anyway. Repent means to turn and go in the opposite direction, a 180 degree turn. What turns do you need to make as you run toward God?

_____

_____

_____

_____

_____

_____

_____

_____

_____

_____

_____

ABOUT THE AUTHOR

Cathy Biggerstaff is passionate about children and the God who creates them. He has called her to write for children, both literature and church curriculum. Cathy's devotions, poems, and articles have been published in print and online. Cathy is the Assistant Coordinator for Community Bible Study in her town, specializing in the areas of Audio/Visuals, blogging and Social Media. She is the Director of the Encouragers Christian Writers Group and is the Financial Director for Write2Ignite! Writers Conference. Cathy shares the Good News of Jesus through "Jewel, the Clown" in a Christian clown ministry.

Her first real trial as a Christian came after the death of her daughter. She clung desperately to this verse from I Corinthians 13:12 (NRSV) – "For now we see in a mirror, dimly, but then we will see face to face. Now I know only in part; then I will know fully, even as I have been fully known." She decided she could hold onto all her questions until that day when God revealed the answers.

As Cathy's faith grew, Jeremiah 29:11 became her hold-on-to verse. Her current life verse is, Isaiah 9:6 (ESV), "For to us a child is born, to us a son is given; and the government (order) shall be upon his shoulder, and his name shall be called Wonderful Counselor, Mighty God, Everlasting Father, Prince of Peace." Jesus is all we need - today, tomorrow and forever.

Contact Cathy via her blog Joyful Journey, or e-mail hiskid410@gmail.com

ABOUT THE AUTHOR

Stella Rome Carroll, formerly an adult Sunday school teacher, now resides in an assisted living home. Her passion has been teaching Sunday school and writing. Even though she is no longer able to attend church she has continued to write an article about her Sunday school class for her church monthly newsletter. This way she remains connected to her Sunday school family. She had felt called to teach Sunday school and experienced more of a loss for her class than any of her possessions. She has found, however, that in the nursing home there is a need for a word of encouragement and prayer for many of the residents so God still uses her passion to spread His love.

She had previously written biographical sketches of pastors from 1912-2012 for The Centennial book for her church, Trinity Baptist Church in Mooresboro, NC. She has also been published in The National Alliance on Mental Illness newsletter in which she wrote a book review about the book "Crazy" by Pete Early.

Rather than buy gifts when she was not able to shop, she compiled a book of pictures and memories for each of her sons. She has also written "Childhood Memories" for both of her sisters for their birthdays in lieu of gifts with fancy bows. In all she has experienced she has learned that in the whole realm of things, her love and devotion for God and His purpose is more important than anything else she could accomplish in life.

Contact Stella at: stellarome@yahoo.com

ABOUT THE AUTHOR

Rachel Critchley lives in the foothills of Western North Carolina. This is a beautiful place where nature gives you magnificent views every day. She is a native North Carolinian who recently moved back to the area where she was raised. Getting reacquainted with the familiar and discovering the unfamiliar has been interesting and fun. Rachel enjoys traveling with her husband. They recently celebrated their thirtieth wedding anniversary. She feels like she is much too young to have been married that long but there are plenty of stories to tell from all those years together.

Rachel recently retired and finds that all of the extra time she thought she would have quickly becomes filled with family, friends and hobbies. She has always had a passion for reading and writing. She now has the time to work on her favorite hobbies, particularly on writing more. When Rachel puts pen to paper, she writes about life with the intent to inspire people. Her style often encourages her readers to think by including a twist that gives the story a whole new meaning. Rachel gets her inspiration from family, nature and God.

Contact Rachel at: rachelcritchley@gmail.com

ABOUT THE AUTHOR

Mary Jane Downs is a retired preschool teacher. She has a heart for children and the desire for them to hear and accept the Gospel of Christ. She has two grandchildren that she loves to spoil. In January, 2016, Mary Jane will be marrying and moving from North Carolina to the mountains of Northwest South Carolina with her new husband and their collection of rescued animals.

For eight years, she has been a member of the Rutherford County Healing Rooms team, a group of intercessors who pray weekly for the physical, emotional, and spiritual needs of those who come for prayer. Mary Jane loves to make quilts of all sizes, hand assembling and hand quilting them. She prays over each one as she quilts them and then enjoys giving them away to family and friends.

Mary Jane's uplifting devotionals and poems are inspired by her everyday life experiences with God and are in print and online. She is the Assistant Coordinator of the Encouragers Christian Writers Group and writes regularly for her blog, Joy in the Morning, which can be found at www.maryjanewrites.com

ABOUT THE AUTHOR

Mary Edwards and her husband, Donnie, moved to the foothills of North Carolina in 1989 and fell in love with what she brags is "God's Country." As a Mother of 4, grandmother of 5, Mary has an abundance of life stories as a writer and blogger.

She is a four year attendee of the Writers Advance! Boot Camp. You can find her written work and examples of her photography in These Foothills Magazine, The Tryon Daily Bulletin and Mature Living Magazine. Mary owns Photos By M.E. Photography and often combines photography and writing.

Mary is a trained speaker through Christian Communicators. Mary is the founder of Be A Voice 4 Kids, a ministry to give hope to victims and survivors of child sexual abuse. She has been the guest speaker at the Chosen Chicks for Christ conference and at "What's in Your Purse?" Mary has been the guest speaker on Christian Devotions SPEAK UP! Blog Talk Radio show and the Stop Abuse Child Abuse Now Bill Murray Blog Talk Radio Show.

With much prayer she followed God's call to become trained as a facilitator of Stewards of Children through Darkness to Light, an organization that strives to help prevent child sexual abuse. Mary loves to share the Love of the Lord and strives to bring hope to those who are thirsty and hungry for what can only be found through Jesus Christ.

Mary and her ministry can be reached through her website: www.beavoice4kids@vpweb.com

ABOUT THE AUTHOR

Annette Gates is a career wife, mother and Grammy, with formal education in nursing. After being married for 38 years, Annette became the solitary member of the Gates One in Christ team, seeking God's answer to the question, "What now?" Living on a little hillside farm in upstate SC caring for her critters, she enjoys spending time with God in this natural haven.

Annette gained a foundational answer to "What now". Her purpose is to love God and through Him to love others. This is supported by a quote from a sister in widowhood, "I'd say you have a heart to reach out and help others (humans as well as animals). Those that meet you instantly become your friend."

With God's encouragement, Annette has found value in life's trials: "He comforts us in all our troubles so that we can comfort others. When they are troubled, we will be able to give them the same comfort God has given us" (2 Corinthians 1:4 NLT).

Annette hopes to accomplish that very thing; encouraging, comforting and helping others via Social Media, greeting cards, letters, personal interaction and prayers.

Annette is a writer, speaker, teacher, and is currently facilitating a scripture discussion group. Writing credits include newsletter writer/publisher, curriculum writer for preschool through adults, children's literature and Christian devotions. Contact Annette by e-mail at: annettegates@hotmail.com.

ABOUT THE AUTHOR

Lorna Hawley is new to writing, but feels God has called her to share the miracles He has exhibited in her family so she is writing her first book about those experiences. Through God's inspiration, she has written several Christian skits which have been performed by and for various groups, including Community Bible Study in her area.

Missions are her passion and it has been her privilege to travel to many countries to share the love of Jesus. She also enjoys spending time scrapbooking the pictures from each trip. During a recent trip God impressed on Lorna that she was there to do something other than what she expected to do on that trip. Opening herself up to God's direction, Lorna spent her time encouraging the mission couple she was visiting: she listened as they bared frustrations; she cared for the children while the parents took a much needed break; and she acted as an encourager. God showed her that sometimes the things we consider little things are what is needed most. Lorna is a retired Obstetric and Pediatric nurse. Serving as a Bible Study leader continues to enhance her spiritual growth. She has four married daughters and eight grandchildren. She is widowed and lives in North Carolina.

Lorna can be reached by email at: hawley_lorna@yahoo.com

ABOUT THE AUTHOR

Pam McCormick is a retired teacher and aspiring writer, who currently tutors math at her local community college. Pam had a story, "The End," published in Isothermal's magazine, "The Mentor," in December, 2014. She is a member of the Encouragers Christian Writers' Group which meets monthly. In her free time, she enjoys watching old timey westerns and hiking with her husband, and visiting her children in New York and Colorado.

Every other Sunday, she visits a nursing home and teaches a Bible study, feeling very blessed by God for this divine opportunity to share her love for her Savior. Pam loves to travel but also enjoys quiet evenings at home reading a good book, working crossword puzzles and grilling out. Pam's favorite snacks include sour worms, popcorn and twizzlers. Although tough times have come along her journey, she finds solace in the truth that God is always there, just a prayer away, ready to lift her back up on her feet and help her start afresh. Watch for the release of her upcoming book series, Celery Stalks and Coffee Grounds, stories based on her life experiences and God's intervention.

You can contact her at pjmc411@gmail.com

ABOUT THE AUTHOR

Carolyn Wease writes with the intent to inspire her readers with a positive message. Her writings are generally lighthearted or inspirational. Her hope is that through her writing she can give an encouraging word or uplifting lesson that points her readers to Christ.

She lives with her husband Mike in the foothills of the beautiful Blue Ridge Mountains of North Carolina where she was born and raised. She surrounds herself with her children and grandchildren, from whom she receives much of her writing inspiration. With eleven grandchildren there is never a lack of resource material.

Carolyn discovered her love for writing after her children were grown and she was continuing her education at the local community college. It was then that it became apparent to her that she was entering another phase of her life and writing would be an important part of it. Carolyn discovered the Encouragers Christian Writers Group through a seminar at the community college. Now, whether in her writing or her personal walk through life, she strives to be a reflection of our Lord Jesus Christ who is the author of the greatest story ever written.

Contact Carolyn by e-mail at: cawease50@bellsouth.net

Made in the USA
Charleston, SC
30 January 2016